FIRST 50 RECORDING TECHNIQUES

YOU SHOULD KNOW TO TRACK MUSIC

by Bill Gibson

ISBN 978-1-5400-5347-3

Visit Hal Leonard Online at
www.halleonard.com

Contact us:
Hal Leonard
7777 West Bluemound Road
Milwaukee, WI 53213
Email: info@halleonard.com

In Europe, contact:
Hal Leonard Europe Limited
42 Wigmore Street
Marylebone, London, W1U 2RN
Email: info@halleonardeurope.com

In Australia, contact:
Hal Leonard Australia Pty. Ltd.
4 Lentara Court
Cheltenham, Victoria, 3192 Australia
Email: info@halleonard.com.au

CONTENTS

PREFACE

Welcome! This work has been specifically designed to provide advice to those who are either new to recording or who have been recording but would like to get better very quickly. This entire "First 50..." concept has been born to teach you more about tracking music in a shorter period of time than most any other book. Each technique is two pages long, which forced me to condense my thoughts and provide just what you need to know to be successful at each technique. And, these are by no means watered-down bits of data with no payoff. The images and text are tightly packed and full of helpful advice and insights.

First 50 Recording Techniques You Should Know to Track Music is about recording drums, bass, keys, acoustic guitar, electric guitar, and vocals. To ensure that this is most helpful, mixing techniques are not included. Instead, this book is all about aiming your creative musical path squarely at success, starting with ways to prepare for tracking that are tested and reliable. If the basic tracks aren't structured and recorded well, then rest of the process is destined to bring disappointment. If you'll heed the advice and learn the techniques in this book, you'll soon see and hear a very positive difference in your recordings. And, you'll soon discover that you are able to capture audio recordings at a new and exciting level.

TECHNIQUE 1
Preparing for Greatness

OVERVIEW: This is the type of resource that is conducive to jumping ahead; however, I seriously recommend reading these initial chapters because they are all about preparing for success. If you're wondering why your recordings never seem to match up to your Grammy-winning favorites, it could very well be due, in part, to the experience invested in preparing for those recordings. Great performers strive to keep everything tuned and prepped to the max. Their instruments are set up by technicians who specialize in removing obstacles to great performances. If an instrument is tuned and adjusted for the best possible sound and optimum playability, great players deliver virtuosic performances. But it's also very important to note that, no matter their level of musical proficiency, every musician benefits from the inspiration and feel of a great instrument that's been set up for success.

CHALLENGE: We can be our own worst enemy when it comes to preparing for success. It takes time and planning to make sure you have new strings on the guitar, new heads on the drums, or that your instrument is set up and ready to inspire a great performance. Avoid settling for "it'll be good enough." Great producers always make sure the instruments are ready for the recording session. If cost is an issue, then do whatever you can to prepare your instrument. Consider it an investment that will pay off over and over. Ten years from now, you don't want to still be cringing at the sound of an out-of-tune guitar or a dead-sounding snare drum on the recording of your band.

SOLUTION: Tune, tune, tune! Tone, tone, tone! Get new strings, new heads, and get your instrument in tune. Sometimes, there's more to getting in tune than simply adjusting the tuning machines on the guitar or bass, or turning the lugs on a drum. Get to know your instrument and learn what it takes to keep it in shape. Here are a few examples of critically important considerations:

1. Tune the strings and tune the neck: Most guitarists learn quickly how to tune the guitar strings—that's important! Tuning aids are helpful. Most digital audio workstations (**DAWs**) provide guitar tuner plug-ins, but for portable use, I've found that Cleartune for the iPhone is rock-solid, and it displays tuning in **cents** (100ths of a half step). But, the intonation of your neck is as least as important as tuning the open strings because that's what controls the intonation of the fretted notes up and down the neck. Almost all electric guitars provide a way to move the bridge pieces forward and back—shortening or lengthening the string. An experienced tech comes in handy here, but it's also a good DIY task. One string at a time, play the harmonic at the 12th fret, then lightly play the fretted note on the 12th fret without bending the string. If the fretted note registers

sharp on your tuner, use the bridge screw for that string to move the bridge piece toward the tail piece, making the distance between the nut and the bridge longer. Or, if the fretted note is flat, move the bridge piece toward the nut, shortening the string. Once you find the bridge piece location where the harmonic and the fretted note at the 12th fret register the same on your tuner, you can trust that the notes up and down the neck will be in tune—unless of course your frets are excessively worn. Definitely call a tech for that fix.

2. Drum tuning is a skill that anyone who tracks music should develop: There are ample online resources to help you tune drums for any genre. However, here are a couple considerations that will help shed additional light on how to get a great drum sound:

It's not always easy to get a pure tone from a mounted tom. The standard tom mounts that have been used on drumsets from the beginning, involve a bracket screwed into the drum shell that hangs on a post mounted to the kick drum. A much better system uses a bracket mounted to a stand that lets the drum hang from four or more lugs. This system doesn't choke the drum tone like the old-school bracket mounts. Most newer high-end kits use these mounts, but adding them to a vintage kit makes a big difference in the way the drum sounds.

Tuning a drum involves adjusting the head to the same tension all the way around the drum. Most drum techs prefer to use their ears to hear the pitches at each lug, tuning them with the drum key back and forth and across the drum until the head resonates perfectly—then they move to the other side. A pure tone is the result of the top and bottom heads being tuned the same, but many drummers prefer to tune the top head slightly higher so that the pitch drops a little just after it is struck. No matter what your preference, drum tuning can be tedious and frustrating for the novice. The Drum Dial is a valuable tuning aid because it measures the head tension at each lug. It lets you see the tension all the way around the drum. If the tension is the same all the way around, then the head is in tune.

TIP: Tune to your touch. If your guitarist plays hard and moves around a lot, keep that in mind when tuning his or her guitar. Aggressively picking a guitar string causes it to start out sharp until it eventually settles into the tuned pitch. If the player strums hard, tune the guitar while playing with equal vigor.

TECHNIQUE 2
The Song

OVERVIEW: If you ask any successful music producer his or her opinion about the most important aspect of a hit recording, you'll find a consistent response: the song. You might find a different answer from someone, but in my experience, the answer to this question is virtually unanimous. A singer might tell you it's the vocal performance that makes a hit or a guitar player might tell you it's the punchy guitar track, but anyone who sees the entire process soon learns that a great song can make even a marginal singer a star... but a bad song is just a bad song.

CHALLENGE: It's difficult to know exactly what makes up a great song, but the one constant among people who write great songs is that they are always writing songs. If you want to be a great songwriter, write songs every day. It's no different than practicing any instrument. In Malcolm Gladwell's *Outliers*, he poses that it takes about 10,000 hours of practice to master a discipline. That theory has its detractors; however, there's a lot of good that can be said about the impact of practice on any area of study. So, get started on your 10,000 hours!

Of course, there are plenty of cases where an artist who has never written a song before comes up with a hit—hooray for Hollywood! But there is also a reason that songwriters such as Diane Warren write hit song after hit song after hit song. It's because they are constantly writing, refining, writing some more, and rewriting their songs.

Songwriting takes time and dedication. Too frequently, an artist or band comes up with 10 songs for a 10-song album. That's a recipe for disappointment. You're better off going through many, many songs to find the 10 best for your recording. Quincy Jones listened to over 800 songs to find the nine songs that made it on Michael Jackson's *Thriller!* They actually recorded nine songs, and then Quincy decided to pick the four weakest songs and beat them with four new songs!

SOLUTION: You might not need to go through 800 songs to find the songs for your album, but you really should have at least two or three times the projected number of songs from which you can choose final selections to be included on the album.

Most active songwriters prefer to work with a co-writer. Songwriting is such a personal and vulnerable activity that it is comforting to run the song by a trusted writing partner. Another perspective is extremely valuable, and your songs will be much more powerful if you work with a co-writer. Find a writing partner who adds strengths to your weaknesses. If you are great with lyrics, then find a partner who is great with melody and chords. For most songwriters, the process of co-writing is much more stimulating and productive than shouldering the entire songwriting load.

It's also a good idea to look elsewhere for songs. Scour your network of musicians. Joining industry organizations like the Recording Academy (the Grammy folks) is a great way to meet people who might need you as much as you need them.

Taxi.com is an excellent resource for songwriters as well as those looking for songs. Songwriters subscribe to Taxi as a doorway to a broad audience of creative professionals who are looking for songs. Taxi will only receive requests for songs from their members, publishers, or other industry professionals with a strong track record for success. If you're working with a reputable manager or label, then they can help you find many song options.

Taxi.com QR code

Great songs tend to share certain characteristics:

1. They have infectious melodic choruses: People can't help but think of the strong hook (the most memorable parts) in the chorus. Songs like the Beatles' "Hey Jude" or Whitney Houston's "I Wanna Dance with Somebody" stick with the listener for a lifetime.

2. They are strong melodically: A great melody in the verse prepares listeners for the chorus.

3. They have compelling lyrics that contain surprises, telling a story in an interesting, fresh, and exciting way: Great songs don't tend to have trite lyrics.

4. They provide contrast: Usually, the verses stay lower and more subdued, and then the chorus is large and anthemic. Sometimes, the bridge is monstrous, and other times it breaks down to a more open texture. Either way, it provides contrast to the verses and chorus.

CHARACTERISTICS OF A GREAT SONG

- Catchy melody

- Strong chorus with an infectious hook

- Very singable and anthemic

- Musical Contrast

- Compellng Lyrics

Hit songs virtually always follow the same basic form. They don't have to, but each part of the song has a purpose, and unless you're a truly great writer with an inspired new approach, it's best to stick to the tried and true form.

Most hits conform to the following song form:

1. Intro: The intro sets the mood for the song, often with an instrumental hook that leads smoothly to the verse.

2. Verse: Verses tell the story of the song. They frequently give insight to the songwriter's soul.

3. Chorus: The chorus is the big part of the song with the most memorable melody and a simple theme that is stated over and over. Choruses shouldn't be too complex or they won't be memorable enough.

4. Verse: Most songs have two verses. The second verse tends to share another glimpse into a different part of the songwriter's soul.

5. Chorus: It's best when Chorus 2 is identical to Chorus 1. The song is still all about the point being made by the chorus, so give your audience a break and don't confuse the point with changes to the chorus.

6. Bridge: The bridge, sometimes referred to as "the middle 8" provides emotional contrast to the verses and chorus. Sometimes it sheds a new lyrical light on the song's message, and other times it is an instrumental solo or musical breakdown.

STANDARD POP SONG FORM

- Intro

- Verse

- Chorus

- Verse

- Chorus

- Bridge

- Chorus (repeat and fade)

---

7. Chorus (repeat and fade): Most recorded songs repeat the chorus and fade out. In a live show, every song needs an ending, but in a recording, the fade tends to leave the listener with the impression that the song is still going on. If it's a great song, it actually is still going on in the listener's heart even though it has left their ears.

TIP: Look to great literary works for songwriting ideas. The authors of classic books are, or were, gifted with words. When reading a great book, you're likely to run across an inspiring idea that you can expand into an interesting and compelling lyric.

TECHNIQUE 3
Preproduction

OVERVIEW: Preproduction could literally be the single most effective contributor to a successful tracking session. Any experienced producer will make sure that preproduction is thorough before taking the artists to the studio. This is especially true when renting a commercial facility because the time there is limited and expensive; however, preproduction is also crucial when tracking in your home studio. There are certain factors that need to be preplanned. That's what preproduction is all about.

CHALLENGE: There's a phrase that's tossed around the recording community that says, "Fix it in the mix." It's so tempting when you're in the middle of a tracking session that lacks preparation, to rely on the mix engineer. Do everything you can to avoid that mindset. Structure the musical parts during preproduction so that they work well together, supporting each other rather than conflicting with each other. The reason A-list session musicians can walk into a recording session cold is because they have become experts at structuring musical parts that support rather than detract. Almost all musicians need the benefit of preproduction.

SOLUTION: The following issues must be addressed and agreed upon during preproduction:

1. Set the song structure: Make sure everyone in the tracking session knows the arrangement and that they have created musical parts that flow smoothly between musical sections. If you decide during the mix that there should be one more chorus at the end of the song, then that can be done by copying and pasting a previous chorus after the existing last chorus. However, the natural flow that's created as each musician builds to the repeat will be missing.

2. Agree on the arrangement: Choose where and when each musician will play so that there is contrast and excellent musical flow. It's a good idea to map out the structure of each song. A simple bar graph is helpful for those who can't read music, but simple charts are extremely useful for those who can read music.

3. Work out all of the vocal harmony parts: Never wait until the session to structure any background vocal parts (**BGVs**).

4. Record rehearsals: Most musicians are excellent at self-directing once they hear themselves play. Make absolutely sure that you record every rehearsal during preproduction and that the whole band listens to the recordings critically.

5. Explore special guitar tunings: It's amazing the difference a unique tuning can make on a guitar part. Alternate tunings and capos can make a big difference in the sound of your recording.

6. Plan out the exact tracks you need during the tracking session and set up the DAW project so that everything is ready to go for the session: Have all of the tracks created, assign the tracks to groups where required, and make sure you've planned out the progress for tracking so you always have enough tracks. Since most affordable interfaces have two, four, or eight tracks, you'll need to have the plan ready that gets the most out of your recording time.

	INTRO	VERSE 1	CHORUS	VERSE 2	CHORUS 2	BRIDGE	CHORUS	CHORUS	CHORUS (FADE)
LEAD VOC		LEAD VOC	LEAD VOC	LEAD VOC	LEAD VOC		LEAD VOC	LEAD VOC	
BGV 1			BGV 1		BGV 1		BGV 1	BGV 1	
BGV 2			BGV 2		BGV 2		BGV 2	BGV 2	
ACOUSTIC GTR	AC GTR	AC GTR		AC GTR			AC GTR	AC GTR	AC GTR
E. GUITAR			E. GUITAR	E. GUITAR	E. GUITAR	E. GUITAR		E. GUITAR	E. GUITAR
SOLO GUITAR	SOLO GTR					SOLO GTR			SOLO GTR
STR PAD	STR PAD	STR PAD		STR PAD				STR PAD	STR PAD
DRUMSET			DRUMSET	DRUMSET	DRUMSET	DRUMSET		DRUMSET	DRUMSET
CONGAS	CONGAS		CONGAS		CONGAS	CONGAS		CONGAS	CONGAS

7. Whenever possible and appropriate, make sure the click track is ready to go: It's a good idea to record a guide track in advance of the tracking session so there's no doubt about where the parts start and stop. A simple reference vocal and scratch guitar track will keep everything in order.

8. Set markers at all of the arrangement sections so it's easy for the engineer to navigate the arrangement.

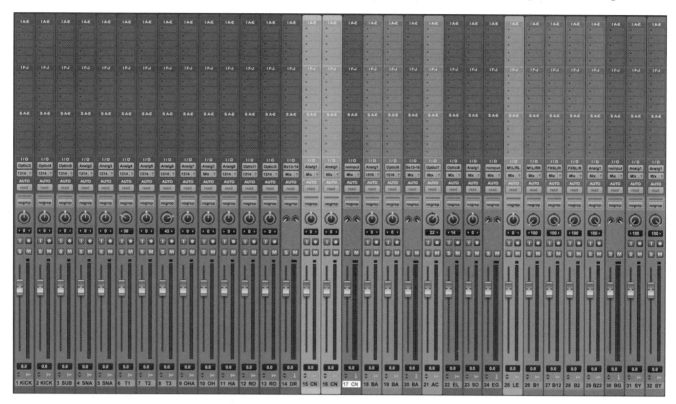

The Pro Tools window above is ready to go for the session. All tracks are created, routed through subgroups where appropriate, panned, and labeled. Only in an emergency is it appropriate to wait until the tracking session starts to get your session ready.

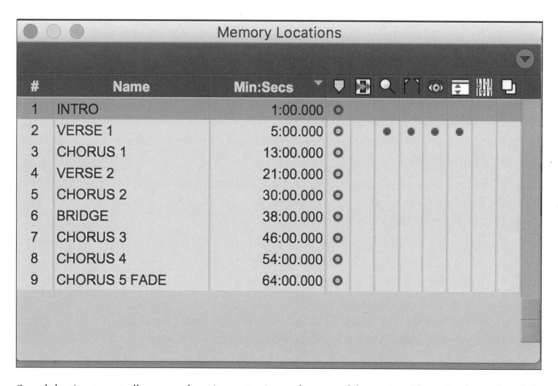

Spend the time to get all memory locations set prior to the start of the session. These simple markers help speed up the session dramatically. Rather than hunting around the session for CHORUS 4, simply click on the memory location named CHORUS 4 and you're instantly in the correct location.

TIP: When using memory markers, set the pre-roll to one or two bars. That way, even though the marker takes you to the beginning of the chorus at bar 30, the musician automatically hears a one or two bar count-off before they begin playing.

TECHNIQUE 4
The Environment

OVERVIEW: Although music is made up of melody, harmony, and rhythm, at its core, music is emotion. Great performers and skilled musicians are truly at their best when they move past technique and into pure emotion. When tracking music, the focus often shifts to the pursuit of technical excellence because, after all, we want to get it perfect, right? Well, we should be able to expect that we can record the performance with the proper levels and without distorting something in the signal path. And, we should be able to expect that the musicians will sing and play skillfully, in rhythm, and in tune. But real music transcends pitch and rhythm. It is really all about conveying emotion, so we need to do whatever we can to inspire an emotional performance.

CHALLENGE: The modern recording process can be extremely unnatural and uncomfortable. We often record things in small bites, never really allowing the space for the musicians to naturally control the energy in their performances. There's nothing less natural for a singer than stopping and starting to punch in this or that note to get it in tune or timed just right. Some singers learn to exist in that kind of environment but that doesn't necessarily mean they thrive in that environment. If we're trying too hard to get musicians, especially singers, to perform notes that please our ears, we're missing the mark. It's much more important to inspire the musicians to deliver emotion to our hearts.

SOLUTION: To get the best possible performances from musicians, create a comfortable environment that sets the perfect atmosphere to support an emotional performance. Get as many details covered as possible to set a good mood for the session.

1. Lighting is crucial: Low light levels, colored lights, spot lights, and candles all set a nice mood. Most commercial studios use heavy duty Variac dimmers that don't induce noise into the audio signal. If you're tracking at home, it's best to make certain that any light circuits with inexpensive dimmers are turned off. Inexpensive dimmers like the ones that are about the size of a regular light switch are electrically noisy, typically causing an annoying buzz in nearby audio signal paths. LED lighting systems with commercial dimmers are a good option. They're very versatile and the low-power LEDs don't produce excessive heat like incandescent and halogen lights.

This kind of dimmer induces a noisy buzz into the audio signal path. Turning the switch off usually clears up the problem.

2. Homey decorations help: Freestanding lamps and area rugs can make a big open studio feel more comfortable.

3. Room temperature is important: Some like it hot; some like it cold. Make sure the artist is comfortable.

4. Keep enough bottled water on hand for everyone: Hydration is important, especially for singers. Just make sure to avoid very hot and very cold choices—both can be problematic on vocal chords.

5. Provide food and snacks: Recording sessions can go on and on. Keep something on hand that suits the musicians and keep an eye on meal times. Lunch and dinner breaks are worthwhile time investments.

6. Using baffles to create a booth for vocalists serves two functions: the smaller space helps make the sound more intimate at the microphone, and a smaller space can be more emotionally comforting than a large, open room.

7. Singers can be especially insecure: If the singer is uncomfortable with a large crowd in the control room, ask everyone to leave. If your singer wants to sing with his or her back to the control room, make it happen. Do whatever it takes to make the singer or instrumentalist comfortable—it makes a difference. Even Michael Jackson preferred to keep all of the lights off except a single pin-spot shining straight down on the microphone!

Variac dimmers are heavy, bulky, and expensive, but they don't cause annoying buzzes in the audio signal.

8. All positions in the room are not created equal: If you're tracking in a large studio, move the source around the room until you find the position that sounds best. In fact, even if you're recording in your family room or garage, move the source around the room to hear the differences in the sound quality. You'll find that the drums in the studio diagram below sound different at each location (1, 2, 3, or 4). You don't even need to set mics up at each position. Just move the drums around until you find the location that sounds best. Then start setting mics up.

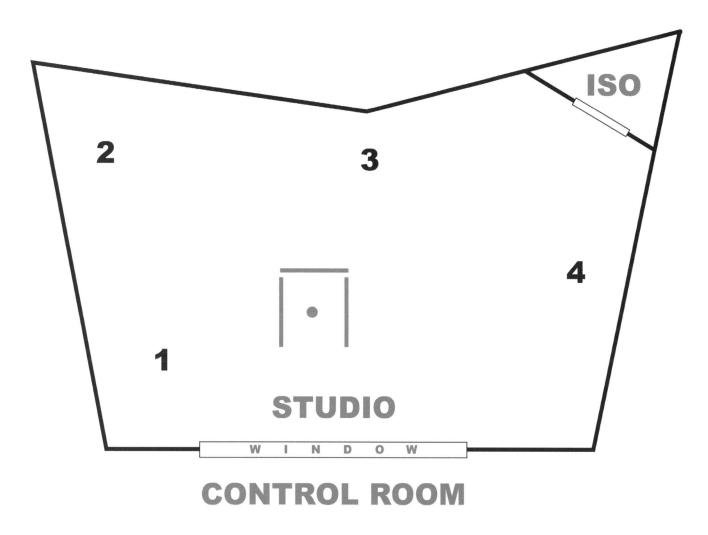

9. Eliminate distractions: Every artist is different. Some love having people watch them perform. Others get self-conscious when they know there are a lot of people watching. It's up to you to be aware of what it will take to get the best performance. Don't be shy about asking girlfriends, boyfriends, or band members to leave the control room when it's time to record.

TIP: Getting the best performance out of any creative person is all about relationship. If you're going to ask someone to be vulnerable and to try things that are outside their comfort zone, they need to know that you're their biggest advocate.

TECHNIQUE 5
The Importance of Studio Acoustics

OVERVIEW: Tracking involves two primary physical acoustical spaces:

1. The studio, which is where the instruments and vocalist perform.

2. The control room, which is where all of the recording equipment is operated by the engineer.

In the studio, if the room sounds bad and the source sounds bad in the room, the recordings made in that room won't sound good. Thankfully, there are many available installed and freestanding acoustic control solutions.

CHALLENGE: Sound bounces around a room in way that's very similar to the way a cue ball bounces around a pool table. Sounds that bounce back and forth between two opposing surfaces (side-to-side, end-to-end, or floor-to-ceiling) can add tonal coloration to recordings captured in the studio.

Acoustical control solutions fit into two broad categories:

1. **Absorbers:** Soft surfaces, such as foam, curtains, blankets, couches, and people absorb high frequencies.

2. **Diffusers:** Low frequencies, below 300 Hz or so, contain significant energy and can't be controlled with simple soft surfaces. This low range can, however, be controlled with diffusers, which interrupt the normal sound wave path, sending it bouncing around the room rather than letting it reflect back and forth between opposing surfaces.

A room with a complex design reflects sound waves around the room. The sound waves lose energy and dissipate before they can cause unwanted coloration. That's why commercial studios, like the one above, are constructed with many interesting non-parallel angles.

Simple spaces such as bedrooms or family rooms (commonly used as home studios) let sound waves form patterns, called "standing waves," that bounce between opposing surfaces. These types of spaces negatively affect the sounds that are recorded in them. Thankfully, there are plenty of manufactured solutions.

SOLUTION: Anything that breaks up a pattern between opposing surfaces in a room is helpful. Deflecting the sound around the room helps smooth out the tonal balance of the room ambience.

There are two very important principles to address when developing a plan to control room acoustics:

1. **Absorption:** Soft surfaces such as foam, drapes, couches, and people absorb sound and help control problematic ambience. However, absorption primarily addresses mid and high frequencies. It's important to note that too much absorption can cause a room to sound dull and lifeless.

2. **Diffusion:** Diffusers redirect sound wave reflections so they travel around the room instead of standing between opposing surfaces. There are many ways to diffuse sound waves, including professionally constructed diffusers, cylindrical columns, hinged wall panels, changing wall angles, and so on. But there are also more organic diffusers such as a large bookcase filled with varying sizes of books—it's even okay to leave some randomly sized spaces between the books.

Controlling acoustical problems is essential, but there are plenty of commercial products available to help. Manufacturers such as Primacoustic, Auralex, and Geerfab make a variety of products, such as this foam wall (right), which absorbs, diffuses, and traps acoustical problems.

Acoustic Sciences Corporation (ASC) builds Tube Traps and Studio Traps that diffuse and absorb sound at the same time—one side of the cylinder absorbs sound waves and the other side diffuses sound waves. If you surround a mic with a set of eight Tube Traps in almost any room, you'll capture a refined, controlled, and appealing sound.

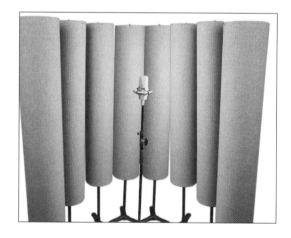

Geerfab manufactures a wide variety of panels that either hang in open space or attach to a wall. A clever implementation of these types of panels can easily tone down acoustical problems in any space.

> **TIP:** Set up a tone oscillator to play tones through any speaker setup in the studio. Set the tone at 50 Hz and walk around the room, taking notice of what you hear. If the room is large, you might be very surprised to learn that at one spot the tone is loud and at another the tone is quiet. Then try 60 Hz, then 70 Hz, and so on.

TECHNIQUE 6
Control Room Monitors

OVERVIEW: It's problematic if the control room monitor system isn't giving you an accurate representation of the sounds you're tracking. The monitoring environment needs to be controlled and the speakers need to be as neutral as possible, neither hyping nor slighting the highs, mids, or lows. If you're making equalization and processing decisions based on bad information, then you'll get bad results.

CHALLENGE: Home recordists frequently used a leftover bedroom or family room for a control room or studio (or both). These types of spaces are less than ideal because they tend to be very simple rooms with parallel side walls and a parallel ceiling and floor—the ideal scenario for tonal colorations and sonic inaccuracies. Rooms designed for recording and monitoring audio typically include non-parallel surfaces and other basic construction features designed to help diffuse and absorb sound.

SOLUTION: It's not the end of the world if the only space you have for recording and monitoring is a simple bedroom or family room, and you can't justify construction costs that could make the space better-suited to recording. Here are some solutions to help overcome control room monitoring problems:

1. Commercially manufactured acoustic control solutions are as useful in the control room as the studio. Foam products like those from Primacoustic and Auralex can be very helpful.

2. Anything that will get in the way of sound waves bouncing back and forth between parallel walls is helpful, so cabinets, large book cases, or equipment racks are good to have around.

3. Simple and free solutions such as pulling the blinds down over the window—this is especially effective with louvered blinds that are slightly tilted open. Or, if there is a closet full of clothes, books, gear, or pretty much anything, leave the door open for a free diffuser/absorber.

4. A set of Acoustic Sciences Studio Traps (the same traps you can use in the studio around a microphone) set up behind the mix position does an amazing job of establishing a trustworthy mixing environment.

Foam squares like these from Primacoustic do an excellent job of breaking up sounds that reflect off the wall behind the mix position. A solution like this won't fix all of the problems, but it will help fix some of the problems.

Large far-field monitors are designed to be 15 or 20 feet from the mix position in rooms that are designed, constructed, and treated to be ideal listening environments. The room is integral to the sound of these monitors.

5. Studio monitors are available in three basic designs: far-field, mid-field, and near-field. Keeping the monitors close to the mix position and monitoring at relatively quiet listening levels minimizes the room's influence on the sound, so the best solution for mixing is to use a set of a near-field reference monitors. Large commercial studios offer far- or mid-field monitors but, even in the best of studios, most mixing is done on near-field monitors, which are designed to be about one meter from the listener's ears and about one meter apart.

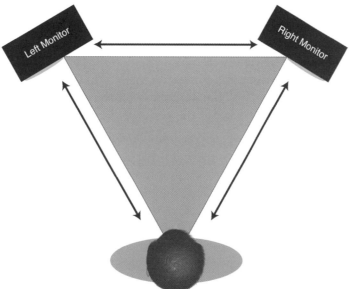

Near-field reference monitors are designed to be used about one meter from the listener's ears and positioned about one meter apart. These monitors keep the sound mostly directed to the listener, diminishing any coloration that the room might be adding.

6. A quiet monitor level doesn't involve the sound of the room in the mix as much as a loud monitor level, so do your best to keep the monitor level around 75 or 80 dB, *C-weighted. You'll find that you can keep turning the volume down as you mix, only occasionally referencing the mix around 90 dB. If the mix sounds good at a quiet level, it will virtually always sound great at a louder level, plus you'll be able to mix for much longer periods of time without ear fatigue when monitoring at low levels.

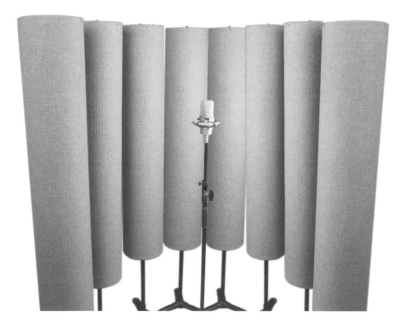

In addition to controlling sound around a mic in the studio, a set of ASC Studio Traps behind the mix position can help make the worst of listening environments trustworthy for mixing.

TIP: Headphones can be a good option if there isn't a reliable room for mixing; however, make sure the headphones aren't hyped in the highs or lows. I like Sony 7506 headphones for tracking but they're too bright for mixing. Headphones like the AKG Q 701 are neutral enough for mixing.

*C-weighted refers to a type of curve used to illustrate data in the measurement of sound pressure levels (SPL).

TECHNIQUE 7
Choosing an Interface

OVERVIEW: With any modern computer and a USB microphone, you can record lots of audio, but only one track at a time. When you connect a USB microphone to your computer, the mic is also acting as the interface. The fundamental purpose of any interface is to convert the analog audio captured by the mic to a digital signal that can be stored on the computer—that's what the USB mic is doing.

Tracking a music project usually involves many scenarios where multiple mics are required. Anytime you need to record multiple channels at the same time, a multi-channel audio interface is required. An interface connects to the computer via USB, FireWire, or Thunderbolt. Even the smallest interfaces provide a couple mic inputs and usually a couple instrument inputs, but the sky's the limit when you need more tracks.

CHALLENGE: As with everything we purchase for audio recording, each of us needs to find the balance between the essentials and the desirables. If you're a solo artist, and your chosen DAW is Reason or Ableton Live, and everything you record includes all virtual instruments and vocals, then you will rarely need more than a single USB microphone. However, if you want to record a drumset or an entire band, then you'll need a larger interface with an increased number of inputs. It's also important to decide if you need the ability to record high-resolution audio. If all of your music is distributed as MP3s or even CD-quality—and that's the way you expect it to stay for the next few years—hi-res audio might not be a necessity. However, the hi-res movement is here now, and the smartest long-term purchases will have the ability to record at up to a 96 kHz sample rate and 24-bit words (96/24) or better.

SOLUTION: Here are some possible solutions based on a few different scenarios:

1. 2 x 2: Interface capacity is typically expressed in two numbers representing inputs X (by) outputs Y. So, a 2 x 2 interface has two inputs and two outputs. These interfaces are useful for many because they have the capacity for stereo miking or for a single mic and single instrument to be recorded at once. Modern interfaces typically use combination input jacks so that each input can be connected to a microphone (XLR) or an instrument (1/4-inch phone). This PreSonus AudioBox USB 96 has two combo inputs, two outputs, plus MIDI input/output (**I/O**) and a headphone jack.

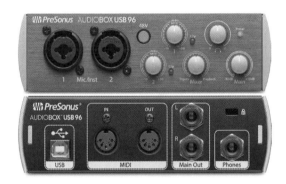

2. 2 x 6: If you're into recording on iOS devices, the iConnectivity AUDIO2+ is a fantastic interface. Like the 2 x 2 interface, it still has two inputs on the front panel but it has six outputs on the back panel (four discrete outputs plus the separate stereo headphone output, all of which can be accessed via internal routing). In addition to the 2 x 6 I/O, this interface has an extra USB jack on the back for connection to an iPad or other iOS device. Therefore, this interface can connect to a laptop or other computer at the same time it connects to the iPad—perfect for integrating sessions that start out on an iOS device but finish up on your main computer.

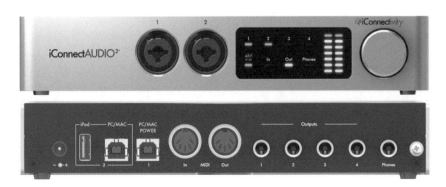

3. 8 x 2: The Apogee Element 88 is a great-sounding interface with lots of potential. Apogee is known for its pristine audio quality and all of their gear sounds fantastic. Functionally, it has eight inputs on the front panel (four combo and four XLR jacks) and two main XLR outputs on the back panel. So, it feels like an 8 x 2 interface; however, it also has two more 1/4-inch balanced outputs on the back panel plus eight channels of optical I/O, and two stereo headphone jacks on the front. The Element 88, like most of the 8 x 8 I/O devices, can be connected in pairs to the same computer via Thunderbolt for double the I/O capacity. The Element series, also available in 2 x 4 and 4 x 6 configurations, is unique because it has no knobs or buttons. All controls are virtual and only available on the computer or iOS interface.

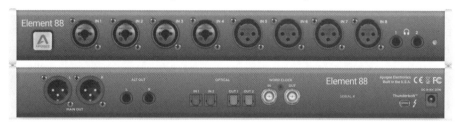

4. 26 x 32: The PreSonus Quantum takes everything to the next level with 26 inputs and 32 outputs. Again, there are only eight actual mic/instrument inputs (all combo jacks) but there are eight discrete balanced 1/4-inch outputs on the back panel, which makes this interface perfect for use in 5.1 or 7.1 surround mixing. Four of these interfaces can be connected to a single system for full 96 x 96 configuration, including 32 mic/instrument combo jacks, 32 discrete 1/4-inch balanced outputs, loads of optical I/O, MIDI I/O, and BNC word clock connections so that all digital devices function in sample-accurate sync.

5. Recording levels: The avoidance of peak levels, where the red light blinks at the top of the meter, is the most important consideration when tracking to a digital recorder. Traditionally, -18 decibels relative to full scale (**dBFS**) equals 0 volume unit (**VU**) (average RMS level). It's most important to avoid overs (peaks) but, especially when recording 24-bit audio, peaking at -6 to -4 dBFS is ample level.

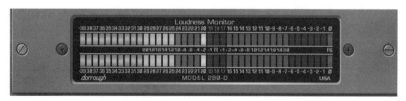

6. A digital mixer connected to a computer via USB, FireWire, or Thunderbolt is also a very powerful and extremely flexible audio interface: The PreSonus StudioLive series offers between 32 and 64 mic/line inputs with full capability to record all channels to a computer and 34 channels to a built-in SD card record/playback device. An interface like the StudioLive provides ample I/O while also giving you fader control over the entire mixdown, plus comparability with Studio One, Pro Tools, and Logic.

TIP: A mixer like the PreSonus StudioLive lets you easily play channels from the multitrack while listening to input channels. This is perfect when a band wants to perform with its own backing tracks or when used for a virtual sound check, letting the sound operator set the FOH and monitor mixes before the band arrives.

TECHNIQUE 8
Managing the DAW

OVERVIEW: At first, you're likely to record some simple projects that are easy to keep track of; however, there will very likely come a day when, all of a sudden, the tracks in your DAW session just get out of control. If you develop good DAW management habits now, then your life will be much more efficient and productive later.

CHALLENGE: It seems like we're always under some sort of deadline, whether corporately or self-imposed. In the hustle of a recording session, it might feel that as the one in charge of the DAW, you can't afford the time to be organized. In reality, you can't afford to not be organized, simply because it's inevitable that the session will eventually bog down, and you'll need to start moving quickly around the session just to keep things going. Every tiny bit of organization will pay huge dividends once that happens—and it surely will happen.

SOLUTION: Here are some habits that you can establish to make your recording life easier and less stressful:

1. Organize your tracks in a consistent order: It doesn't matter so much what the order is, but it is very helpful if you can set an order of tracks and keep it. I like to work down from the top starting with the kick drum mic(s) and then through the snare, toms, overheads, hi-hat, and room mics. Then I like to go to the bass guitar direct input (**DI**) and/or mics, guitars, keys, vocals, and backing vocals with the master fader on the bottom. Use whatever order you want, but keeping it the same from session to session will save you time.

2. Color code the tracks: Virtually every DAW provides a way to color code tracks. Simply making the drums one color, the guitars another, keys, vocals, and so on, provides an excellent visual structure when you're navigating a session. Once you've chosen the colors for the tracks, the faders will also show up in the same colors.

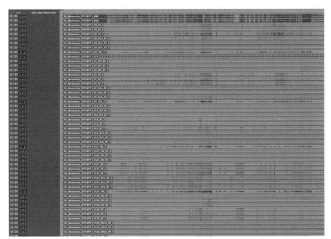 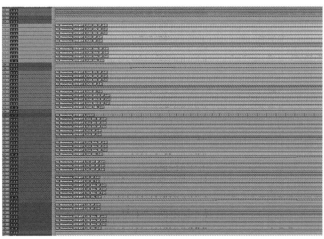

Even in this thumbnail view, clearly the window on the right is much easier to navigate than the window on the left.

3. Track folders, track stacks, and hide/show tracks are a convenient way to collapse tracks out of view. This is especially useful as track counts increase. Studio One (A) calls this feature "Track Folders." Simply select the tracks you want to add to a folder and right-click or control-click to select "Track Folders." Logic Pro calls the same feature "Track Stacks" (B), which is chosen with the same routine. Pro Tools doesn't have a track folder feature; however, they let the user select any number of tracks, and with a right-click or control-click, hide (C) those tracks without disabling them.

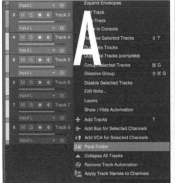  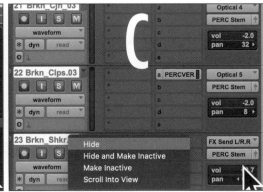

4. Groups, subgroups, and voltage and digitally controlled amplifier (**VCA/DCA**) groups are extremely useful during tracking and mixdown: Almost all DAWs facilitate each of these kinds of control, which in turn, provide simple control over several track faders at once. Any selected faders can be grouped so that moving a given fader adjusts the levels of all the faders in the group (A). Subgroups route the actual audio from a group of faders through an auxiliary fader (B). The advantage to this technique is that the actual audio output of the entire group can be processed, often by a compressor or peak limiter. VCA and DCA groups are also very powerful. They let the user select a group of faders to be controlled by the VCA/DCA master fader (C). Whereas a simple group responds to the touch of any fader in the group, the VCA group level is controlled by the VCA fader, but the individual channels can be adjusted separately—also, channel automation stays active and adjusts relative to VCA fader movements.

5. Markers (memory locations) are extremely useful for navigating the arrangement: There's nothing that will slow down the creative flow more than constantly poking around the session to figure out where the second verse, third chorus, or the bridge is in the song. Anyone should be able to call out any musical section, and the engineer should be able to go exactly there in an instant. Markers are designed to facilitate that kind of navigation. In Pro Tools, for example, hitting the Enter key sets a marker. Simply play through the song and hit Enter at each new section. There's usually enough time to label the section before the next musical section comes around.

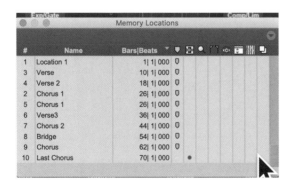

TIP: Always spend time getting everything about the DAW session ready well before the session start time. It's comforting to know that the DAW is ready to go and the mics are all set up. There are enough details to conquer at the start of the session without having to prep the DAW and set up the mics.

TECHNIQUE 9
Choosing the Right Microphone

OVERVIEW: The microphone you choose makes a big difference in the quality of the sounds you capture. Many recording industry icons use mic choice and technique to get the sounds they know they'll need in the mix. They steer clear of equalization (**EQ**) and compression altogether. Listen to the work of Bruce Swedien (Michael Jackson, Quincy Jones, Count Basie, Duke Ellington, and many more) and Al Schmitt (Diana Krall, Paul McCartney, and Bob Dylan among others). Both of these engineers are extreme minimalists when it comes to using EQ and compression.

CHALLENGE: It takes a lot of experience to know what sound you'll need from a voice or instrument in the mix during tracking. But, that should be a goal in the recording process. Moving a mic closer to the source results in an increase in low frequencies. Moving the mic away from the source results in a decrease in low frequencies. So, finding just the right distance from the source for the ideal balance of highs and lows is critical to the quality of the recorded sound. However, the room that the sound is captured in also plays an important role in the sound quality. At first, if you don't have access to rooms that sound great, it might be necessary to move in closer to the source to minimize any undesirable coloration from the room acoustics. Even though it might not be practical at first to use mic technique to get exactly the sound you want, this should still be what you strive for in your recordings.

SOLUTION: Using the best mic for the recording task is very important. For recording, there are three commonly used mic types: **dynamic** (moving-coil), **condenser**, and **ribbon**.

1. Dynamic microphones are typically designed for use close to the source: A principle called the **proximity effect** is demonstrated when a microphone moves closer to a sound source and low frequencies become relatively stronger compared to the high frequencies. In other words, when a microphone moves closer to a source, the sound it captures gets more bass-heavy. Microphones designed for miking in close proximity to the source (within a few inches) have a built-in frequency response that's weak in the low end to flatten out those frequencies as the mic moves closer to the source. Dynamic mics are the most rugged of the mic types, and their capsule design is bulkier than the other common types. They don't respond as well to intricacies in sound waves, especially to **transients** (fast attacks) like those from a percussion instrument. Dynamic mics aren't a good choice for miking a symphony orchestra; however, they're very durable, and they can faithfully handle a lot of volume. They are an excellent choice for miking kick drum, snare drum, toms, guitar and bass speaker cabinets, and close-miked vocals, especially in a live show. The Shure SM57 and SM58 are dynamic microphones, and are the most commonly used microphones of all time.

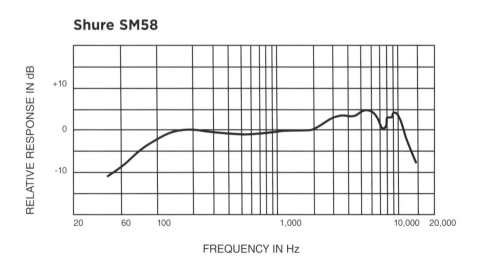

Shure SM58

The line on the SM58 frequency response chart above shows a decrease in the low frequency response. Moving this mic close to the source increases the low frequencies, effectively flattening out the low-frequency response. Also, notice an increase in the high frequencies between about 2 kHz and 10 kHz. This boost in the highs helps increase vocal intelligibility and also helps close-miked drums and guitars cut through the mix. The SM58 (right) has a built-in windscreen and is the music industry's most commonly used vocal microphone.

2. Of the commonly used mic types, condenser microphones are capable of capturing the finest transient detail and waveform intricacies: Whereas the dynamic mic capsule is a little bulky, the condenser capsule uses a very thinly coated plastic membrane to respond to sound waves. Since this capsule is fast and accurate, condenser mics are a first choice for acoustic instruments such as acoustic guitar, piano, strings, woodwinds, and vocals in the studio. They don't typically roll off as much in the low frequencies, and they don't tend to have the hyped high-frequency sensitivity like we see in the frequency response of the SM58. Condenser capsules have either large diaphragms or small diaphragms. Small diaphragm condensers have the flattest response of all mic types, and large diaphragm condensers, which are still relatively flat, are a little warmer-sounding than the other most commonly used studio vocal mics.

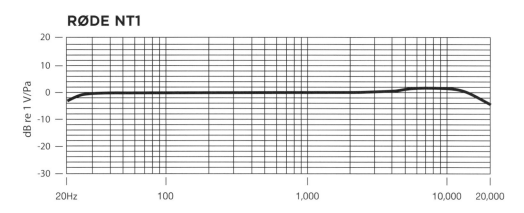

The Røde NT1 has a very flat frequency response graph with a slight roll-off at 20 Hz and a gentle high-frequency bump between about 5 and 15 kHz. Not only is a mic like this is an excellent choice for capturing accurate transients and waveform detail, but also for capturing the sound source from distances of a foot or more. Condenser mics like this often include a high-pass filter so they can be used in close proximity to the source without capturing an overly boomy sound.

3. The strength of modern-day ribbon microphones is their warm, smooth sound quality: The most fragile of the mic types, the ribbon capsule uses a thin metal ribbon suspended in a magnetic field to capture audio waves. Modern ribbon mics are much more durable than classic ribbon mics from the '40s and '50s, so they are a trusted choice, even in the live sound industry. The mic manufacturer Royer introduced a modern version of ribbon microphones in 1998. With the increasing popularity of digital recording, engineers continue to seek the warmth that has been lost in the passing of the analog tape era. On any sound that has a high-end grind, such as distorted electric guitar, brass, and strings, ribbon mics are a fantastic choice, providing a sound that is easy on the ears.

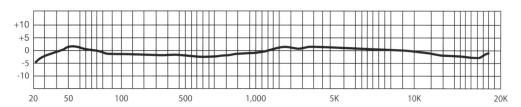

Today, most manufacturers have created their own ribbon mic offerings. The ribbon mic capsule isn't quite as accurate as the condenser capsule, but some say it responds to sound more like the human ear. A modern ribbon mic has a frequency response that's relatively constant across the audible spectrum. The frequency response graph above is for the Royer R-121 (shown right). With their smooth, warm, and appealing sound, which is similar to the warmth and tone of analog tape, modern ribbons have been quickly embraced by the audio industry.

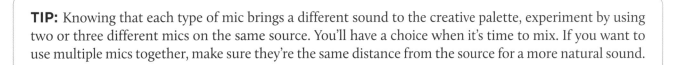

TIP: Knowing that each type of mic brings a different sound to the creative palette, experiment by using two or three different mics on the same source. You'll have a choice when it's time to mix. If you want to use multiple mics together, make sure they're the same distance from the source for a more natural sound.

TECHNIQUE 10
Microphone Polar Patterns

OVERVIEW: A very important microphone specification is the **polar pattern**, a visual representation of microphone directionality. Some microphones pick up sounds equally from all directions. To put it another way, they don't discriminate against sounds coming from any direction. Other microphones capture sounds that are in front of the mic (the part of the mic that's aimed at the source), but they have a reduction in ability to capture sounds behind the microphone (the part that is 180 degrees away from the source). Some microphones capture sounds equally from the front and the back but reject sounds from the sides.

CHALLENGE: Each different polar pattern captures a different sound from the same source in the same acoustic space. Learning to optimize the use of mics with different polar patterns is an important part of any effort to build tracking skills. It takes practice and experience to get the most out of any selection of microphones. It's widely accepted that the best approach to recording music is to choose the best microphone for the job and to use excellent mic technique to capture the most musical and highest-quality sound from the source. Choosing the polar pattern is an important part of that process.

SOLUTION: The first step in using polar patterns to capture great sounds during tracking is to understand what they are and how they are expected to help an engineer record great-sounding tracks. Polar patterns are represented by two-dimensional drawings of the basic pattern, but it is understood that each 2D illustration represents an actual spherical, three-dimensional polar pattern. It's important to note that polar patterns are often indicated with a range of frequencies on the same graph. Even though a mic has a heart-shaped polar pattern at 1 or 2 kHz, it might have an omnidirectional polar pattern at 10 kHz. It's important to review the polar graph carefully to get a complete idea of what to expect from a microphone.

1. **Omindirectional:** An omindirectional microphone doesn't reject sound from any direction in a 360-degree sphere around the mic capsule. Omni mics are a great choice for tracking a group of singers or instrumentalists at the same time to a single track. Carefully position the musicians around the mic to get the best balance. With backing vocals or other small portions of the production, track the same group twice to separate tracks and pan them apart for a great stereo sound. Omnidirectional mics are a frequent choice for room mics, and if the room sounds fantastic, some engineers prefer to use a lot of omni mics in close proximity to the sources where other mics might be a typical choice.

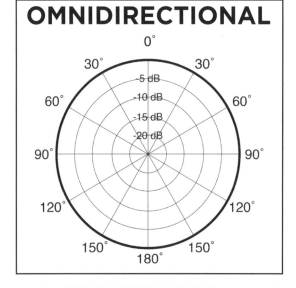

2. **Cardioid:** A cardioid polar pattern is heart-shaped. It captures sound best from the front of the mic but rejects sounds from the back of the mic. Polar patterns are represented by a 360-degree circle, with zero degrees being the front of the mic and 180 degrees the back of the mic. A cardioid mic favors the front of the mic, and is said to have 180-degree, off-axis discrimination because there is an area of decreased sensitivity 180 degrees behind the front of the mic. Cardioid mics are useful because they can be aimed at the source, and also because they can be aimed away from any source that needs to be minimized during tracking.

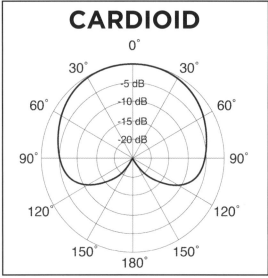

3. **Bidirectional:** A bidirectional microphone captures sound equally at the front and back (zero and 180 degrees); however, there's an effective null at the sides of the mic (90 and 270 degrees). Use a bidirectional mic to record two singers at once, placing one singer at zero degrees and the other singer at 180 degrees. It is especially useful that the sounds arriving at the sides of the mic are rejected very effectively.

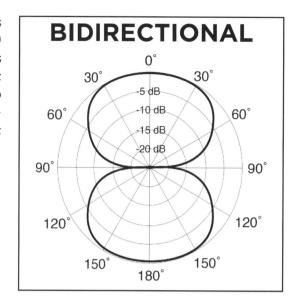

4. **Supercardioid:** A microphone with a supercardioid polar response is more directional at the front than a microphone exhibiting a cardioid pattern, with a decreased sensitivity on the sides and an area of decreased sensitivity about 170 degrees off-axis.

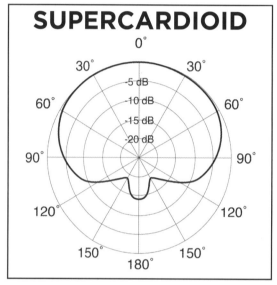

5. **Hypercardioid:** A microphone with a hypercardioid polar response exhibits a high degree of directionality at the front with a decrease of about 12 dB on the sides and the least sensitive area at about 110 degrees off-axis.

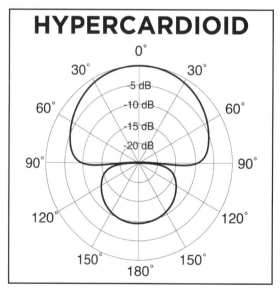

TIP: Microphones with an omnidirectional polar pattern can be positioned very close to the source without capturing a boomy, bassy sound, unlike microphones with a cardioid or bidirectional polar pattern that capture a very bass-heavy sound when positioned in close proximity to the source. Try recording a lead vocal in very close proximity using an omni mic—be sure to use a windscreen.

TECHNIQUE 11
Stereo Mic Techniques

OVERVIEW: A single microphone can be very effective at capturing a great sound, especially in a close-miking application. However, humans use a two-ear design to listen to sound, so there are advantages to using two microphones to record audio, especially for sounds that are traditionally heard in an acoustical space like a concert hall. Combining mono and stereo tracks is a very powerful way to establish an impressive sound field.

CHALLENGE: Learning when to use stereo mic techniques versus mono mic techniques can take a little time, but it usually comes down to the size of the source and how stable the track needs to be in the mix. It doesn't make any sense to use a stereo mic technique on toms, snare, and kick drum because those sounds need to be positioned very specifically in the mix. But it does make sense to use a stereo mic technique for the overheads and room mics to add space and size to the drum sound. It doesn't make sense to record a lead vocal with a stereo mic configuration because the singer would constantly be altering the left-right positioning by moving around. However, tracking a large or small choir with a stereo mic technique makes perfect sense. The listener gets a sense of the acoustical environment in which the choir was tracked.

SOLUTION: As we continue, we'll see different mono and stereo techniques that provide excellent results, so it's important to reference the following standard stereo miking techniques. In most applications, it's very important that the stereo image collapses, or **sums** to mono in a way that still sounds full and clean. Simply setting two mics randomly is likely to capture an image that sounds thin and hollow in mono, even if it sounds huge in stereo. This used to be extremely important when mono AM radio and television were the norm, but today the primary consideration is what the recordings sound like if they're played through a mono live sound system. It can be heartbreaking when you toil over a mix that sounds fantastic in stereo but, when played at a live gig over the sound system, it sounds small and weak because some of the big stereo sounds don't sum faithfully to mono.

1. **X-Y:** The X-Y technique is a very popular choice because it provides a very accurate stereo image while summing very well to mono. It is a **coincident** technique because the two mic capsules are located on the same vertical and horizontal plane and are positioned as close together as possible without touching. The fact that the two capsules are so close together means that they capture sound waves in the same phase relationship so they sum to mono perfectly. The X-Y technique, as with most stereo mic techniques, typically captures sound from a distance of more than a foot or two. Small- or large-diaphragm condenser microphones are commonly used for the X-Y technique.

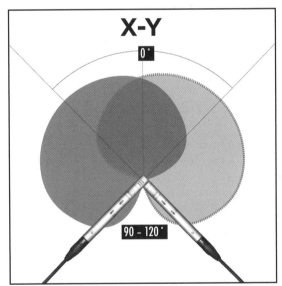

2. **ORTF:** The stereo mic technique developed by the *Office de Radiodiffusion Télévision Française* (ORTF) provides a realistic stereo image that's slightly wider than the standard X-Y configuration. This technique produces excellent results when using two high-quality cardioid condenser microphones. The mics should be aimed 90–110 degrees apart, separated by 17 centimeters (6.7 inches). Whether using the ORTF or X-Y techniques, special mounting brackets help facilitate accurate and repeatable positioning of the mics.

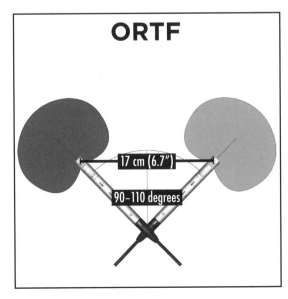

3. **Spaced Pair:** Place two omnidirectional mics in front of the source, spaced between 3 and 10 feet apart. This technique produces a very good stereo image, especially in a room with excellent acoustics. A spaced omni pair is best when used for recording, but in a live sound application, the omnidirectional mics would cause problematic feedback. When recording a small group, such as a vocal quartet, keep the mics about three feet apart. For larger groups, increase the distance between the microphones. A variation of the spaced omni pair uses a baffle between the two mics, which increases the stereo separation and widens the image.

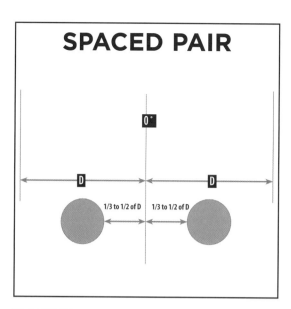

4. **Blumlein:** The Blumlein technique is a coincident technique because the mic capsules are very close together and on the same plane. This technique uses two bidirectional mics in an X-Y configuration, so when summed to mono, the sound isn't significantly degraded. The sound produced by this technique is similar in separation to the X-Y configuration, but with a little more acoustical life.

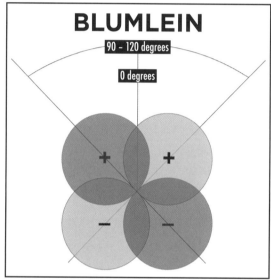

5. **Mid-Side:** The mid-side (MS) technique uses a bidirectional mic positioned with its side aimed at the source along with a cardioid mic aimed at the source. The bidirectional (sides) mic signal is split and sent to two separate channels that are hard panned to the left and right. Then the polarity of one of those channels is reversed for a wide stereo image. The mid (cardioid) mic is blended with the side channels for a natural-sounding stereo recording. When summed to mono, the two side channels completely cancel each other because they are opposite in polarity, resulting in a pure and clean sound from the mid cardioid mic.

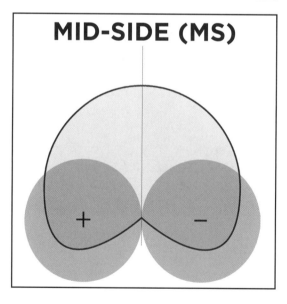

TIP: Adhere to the **3:1 rule** any time multiple mics are being used in the same acoustical environment. Make sure that the distance between any two mics is at least three times the distance from each mic to its intended source. This will help achieve adequate separation and minimal phase problems.

TECHNIQUE 12
Miking the Kick Drum

OVERVIEW: The sound of the drumset in any recording defines the genre. It establishes the energy and gives the listener insight into the musical encounter they're about to experience. What's more, the sound of the kick drum, also called the bass drum, is especially foundational to the stylistic sound of the kit. The way the kick drum is miked determines the potential of recorded sound that eventually ends up in the mix.

CHALLENGE: A little informed technique can go a long way when it comes to getting close-miked drums to sound defined and full. Isolation, separation, and control during mixdown are important, but they're not the only important considerations. It is fundamentally important to use good technique to capture great sounds. And whenever possible, it's a good idea to record multiple mics on the kick drum during tracking to provide options when it comes time to commit to the final kick drum sound during mixdown.

SOLUTION: Most kick drums have a hole in the front head that provides access for microphones to be placed inside the drum, which is where you'll find lots of opportunities for achieving a good solid kick sound. Once you have the mic inside the kick drum, there are two principles to remember:

1. Point the mic at the spot where the beater of the bass drum pedal hits the drum head for the clearest attack.

2. Point the mic toward the shell for a more resonant tone.

The sound you're looking for can usually be found by moving the mic around inside the kick drum between the shell and the point where the beater hits the head. It's best to have a helper move the mic while you listen for the sound that fits the music best.

Since the kick sound is so definitive, and the range of appropriate sounds so diverse, the best sound might be just outside the drum or a few feet away from the drum. These two photos demonstrate some well-tested ideas for capturing a great kick drum sound:

Notice the mic to the left is inside the kick and aimed at the point where the beater strikes the head. This approach provides a sound with the clearest attack.

The mic below is aimed toward the shell, which is the location that provides a more resonant tone.

Ask a helper to move the mic between these two locations to find the sound that works best for the music you're recording.

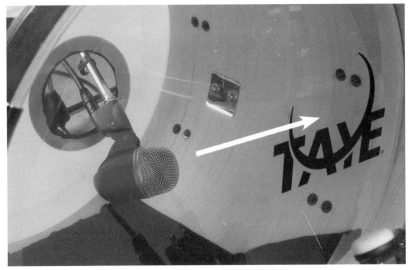

The kick drum to the left is being miked from the front of the head rather than from inside the drum. This approach doesn't provide as much isolation compared to miking inside the kick and the resulting sound isn't typically as tight and punchy. For some genres, such as jazz and other more organic styles, this technique captures the perfect sound for the music.

If there are enough available channels, it never hurts to give yourself some options for mixdown. On this kick drum, I used a Shure Beta 52 inside the kick, a classic Sony C-500 large-diaphragm condenser mic on the outside (the light-colored mic with the large head), and a very cool subkick mic called the "LoFrEQ" from Solomon Mics (the mic that looks like a tiny snare drum on the short stand). If you record each mic to a separate track, then you can blend them together for a great sound when it's time to mix. The mic inside provides a nice attack, the outside condenser mic provides a great tone, and the LoFrEQ provides a great low-end boom.

TIP: If the kick drum tone has too much ring, place something soft inside the drum such as a packing blanket, down pillow, or even a puffy jacket. Let it lean just enough on the batter head to get the tight and punchy sound you want. Use a mic stand base or a cinder block to lock everything in place.

TECHNIQUE 13
Miking the Snare Drum

OVERVIEW: The kick and snare drum provide the energy to the engine that drives the groove. A great drummer and a great drum sound are non-negotiable when it comes to creating a first-class musical production. When it's time to track the drummer, we can't always choose the drums or the drummer, so it's entirely possible that we might end up with a problem that will last the duration of the production process.

CHALLENGE: There are plenty of ways to make a mediocre drum performance work for the music, but that takes a lot of time and skill. The best plan is to set yourself up for success with the best possible drum recordings. Tuning the snare drum is extremely important. If you're going to be effective when tracking drums, you should get familiar with drums and tuning techniques. Hopefully, the drummer will have everything ready to go, but you can't rely on that. The acceptable range of snare drum sounds is extremely wide and is always driven by the music.

SOLUTION: Getting it right from the drummer to the drum, the muffling, and the miking and EQ techniques will set you up for success. Here are some very important considerations:

1. Tuning and muffling are critical: Typically, the top and bottom snare heads will match pitch and work together, with the snares on the bottom head for a clean pop sound. It's also very common to lay cloth on the top of the snare head or to tune one lug all the way down and to even use duct tape, a wallet, or Moon Gel to muffle the top head—it's all about finding the best sound for the music. There are definitely snare sounds that don't require muffling, but most of the time, muffling the top head is very helpful in shaping just the right sound. I like using gel pieces like Moon Gel or SlapKlatz because they're so quick, easy, and flexible, but I've also been at this long enough to trust a good drummer and to never be negative about trying a different snare sound.

2. Microphone choice and technique are fundamentally important: The standard mic choice for the top of the snare drum is the Shure SM57 or one of its cousins, such as the Shure SM58, Beta 57, Beta 56, or possibly a similar dynamic mic. Dynamic mics are a good choice because they can handle a lot of volume without overdriving, they work well in close proximity, they're durable so they can take a beating from the drummer, and they have a built-in presence peak that supports a crisp snare sound.

3. Aim the top mic at the location where the stick hits the head for the clearest attack and cleanest sound: Aiming the mic almost straight down at the head can result in a sound that's a little too thick in the low and low-mid frequencies and lacking clarity in the high end.

Notice that the mic on the top head, a Shure Beta 56 (the same as a Beta 57 on a swivel mount), is aimed across the head at the point where the stick hits. This approach results in a much cleaner and clearer snare tone than when the mic aims almost straight down at the head over the hoop. In fact, we position the mics close to the heads because we need isolation in most cases, but the best drum sounds are achieved when the mics are farther above the head but still pointed where the stick hits.

4. In addition to tuning the snare drum for the sound that best fits the music, make sure that the actual snares—the spiraled wires that press against the bottom drum head—are in good shape, evenly tensioned, and that there aren't broken or loose snares randomly rattling under the drum. If there is a loose or broken snare, just cut it off with wire cutters to eliminate any unwanted rattles.

5. It's a very popular technique to place a second microphone underneath the snare drum aimed up at the snares. This captures the edgy, raspy sound from the snares rattling against the bottom head, and it lets you blend the fuller sound from the top microphone with the thinner snare sound from the bottom microphone. When using a bottom mic on the snare, it is extremely important that you reverse the **polarity**—also commonly referred to as **inverting the phase**—of the bottom mic relative to the top mic! Since the bottom mic points up and the top mic points down, the two are 180 degrees out-of-phase. If you combine the two without inverting the polarity on the bottom mic, the resulting sound, when combined, will be very thin and weak. However, as soon as you invert the polarity of the bottom mic, the sound fills out, and the bottom and top mics will work together for a very nice snare sound. Simply adjust the level of the bottom mic for the preferred amount of snare sound.

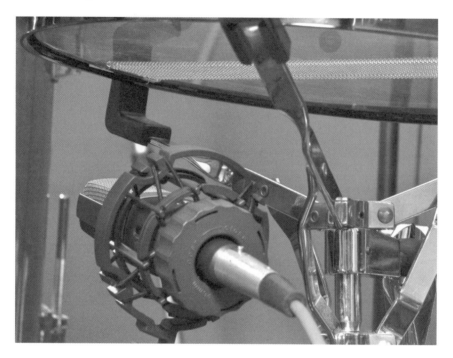

6. Some engineers prefer to use a Shure SM57 on the bottom of the snare because it can naturally handle a lot of volume and because it a has a built-in presence peak that highlights the snare sound. Other engineers like to use a condenser mic on the bottom because of its ability to cleanly capture the extreme transients created by the snares rattling on the bottom head. When using a condenser mic on the snares, make sure that the mic can handle a lot of volume without overdriving and apply any pads that are resident on the mic body.

Notice that the -20 dB pad is engaged on this AKG 214 condenser microphone. It's important to apply the pad whenever you're using a condenser mic underneath the snare drum.

TIP: The drumstick size affects the snare drum sound. Most drummers find a stick they prefer, but if you're looking for a lighter, brighter sound, then use a lighter-weight stick. If you're seeking a heavier tone, try a heavier stick. Also, nylon tips give a much brighter sound than wood tips, especially on cymbals.

TECHNIQUE 14
Miking Toms

OVERVIEW: Toms serve multiple purposes within the drumset. Sometimes they're used as a key component in the actual drum groove, where the left and right hands play a pattern on the toms instead of on the hi-hat, snare, and cymbals. However, the toms are most frequently used to lead the listener from one song section to the next. For example, when moving from the verse to the chorus, a well-played tom fill bridges the listener's attention span, helping them to stay connected to the music and drawing their focus to the chorus.

CHALLENGE: Toms must sound full, clean, and powerful. But it can be problematic in that close-miking a tom, although optimal for isolation, is not really the best way to get a great tom sound. The close-miked drum sound typically contains an overabundance of the frequencies in the 300–600 Hz range. Mic choice and placement can help minimize this problem, but one way or another, the toms need to sound powerful and clean.

SOLUTION: During tracking, we do everything possible to get the best tom sounds recorded. In the days of analog tape, it was important to equalize the tom mics on the way to the recorded track, specifically adding high-frequency boosts to emphasize the attack and carving out low mids to clean up the overall sound. Unfortunately, adding high frequencies during mixdown exaggerated the resident tape hiss.

In today's digital world, it's preferable to save all equalization and other processing for mixdown, using drum tuning, mic choice, and mic technique to capture the best possible raw sound during tracking. Here are several considerations that are useful when tracking toms:

1. Head choice: The head that you choose has an incredible impact on the drum sound. Even if you're not a drummer, you should spend some time learning about different drum heads and what they're advertised to sound like. The thickness of the head, as well as the coating or lack of coating, makes a big difference. There are two-ply heads that help even out the tone, and there are also mesh-web heads. In addition, always use new or nearly new heads when tracking. A head that is well used and stretched out at the point where the stick hits is very unlikely to produce an excellent tone for recording.

2. Tuning: It should go without saying, but any drum that doesn't sound good acoustically has a tough pathway to sounding good when recorded—not that it can't be done, but everything works much better when the drum is tuned. When struck, a tuned drum results in a pure tone without a lot of unattractive overtones. Many drummers tune the top and bottom heads to the same pitch, working hard to make sure the tension and pitch are perfectly even when tapping around the head near each lug.

3. Muffling: Even when a tom is tuned to perfection, muffling is often helpful. A little muffling helps control the ring of the head and definitely helps calm unwanted overtones. I like to use Moon Gel or SlapKlatz because they're both extremely quick and easy to apply, and you can use as little or as much as it takes to get the job done. I'll often tear one gel piece in half and place it out near the rim. A lot of Ringo Starr's drum sounds with the Beatles used tea towels positioned over all or part of the drum head. Many drummers have used duct tape on the heads to get excellent sounds.

4. Mic choice: Dynamic mics are a great choice for miking toms because they can withstand a lot of volume without breaking up, and because they tend to have a built-in presence peak that emphasizes the attack of the stick against the head. The Shure SM57, Beta 57, and Sennheiser 421 MD are the most common choices for dynamic mics on toms. Large-diaphragm condenser microphones such as the AKG 451 and Neumann U-87 are also very popular tom mics because they capture a clean, clear transient and warm tone. Beware that toms are loud, so it's important to select the built-in pad when tracking any drum with a condenser mic.

5. Top mic position: Aim the mic at the point where the stick hits the head to capture the greatest amount of attack. Aim the mic down at the head just inside the rim for more tone. For the greatest amount of isolation, position the tom mics within an inch or two for the head; however, this isn't typically where the best sound is. The best tom sounds are usually found with the mic five or six inches above the head aimed down at the point where the stick makes contact with the head. When tracking drums, it's crucial to listen to the toms in context with the rest of the band and to make any necessary adjustments to capture the sound that best suits the music.

6. Bottom mic position: On large tracking sessions where there are plenty of available tracks and mics, it's common to mic the bottom tom heads in addition to the top. Dynamic mics such as the Shure SM57 and Sennheiser 421 MD are commonly used for this purpose. The bottom mic can provide additional tone and interest in the tom sound, but, as with the bottom snare mic, be certain to reverse the polarity (invert the phase) of the bottom mic. If the bottom mic isn't inverted, then the sound of the top and bottom mics together will be thin and hollow-sounding. Once the polarity is reversed on the bottom mic, its sound is very useful in augmenting the top mic. Consider the bottom tom mic a luxury. A lot of fantastic drum sounds have been captured with just a single mic above the tom.

TIP: Tear or cut an old bed sheet or pillow case into .5- to 3-inch strips. Remove the head and place a strip lightly across the drum at approximately half to two-thirds of the way from the center of the drum to the rim. Replace the head, and as you tighten the lugs, occasionally pull the strip to tighten for a warm, smooth tone. Adjust the strip position and width until you find the perfect sound.

TECHNIQUE 15
Overheads and Hats

OVERVIEW: The overhead and hi-hat microphones fill out the sound of the drum kit. Typically, for a close-miked setup, the kick, snare, and tom mics capture the attack and tone of the drums while the overheads capture the brightness of the cymbals and the fullness of the kit. Also, the hi-hat mic captures the attack and tone from the hats. However, sometimes there aren't enough tracks or mics, so the overheads might be the only mics available, possibly along with a kick and/or snare mic. For the sake of this technique, we'll assume that the drums are being close-miked.

CHALLENGE: Among audio engineers, there are differing opinions about the best way to use overheads. Some—probably the majority—like to get the close mics (kick, snare, and toms) set so they sound great together. Then, they'll blend in the overheads to fill in the cymbals and the overall drum set sound. Other engineers prefer to establish a great overall balance of the drumset with the overheads before turning up the close mics. These engineers move the overheads until they find the position that captures the best-sounding drum balance, after which they fill in the sound of the drums with the close mics.

SOLUTION: Some of the most iconic audio engineers start building the drum sound with the overheads; however, it's important to keep in mind that these engineers work in the best studios on the planet—studios that have great-sounding rooms that augment the drum sound in a positive way. But if you're not recording in the best-sounding rooms, it might not be the best idea to highlight the room sound. So getting a great sound on the kick, snare, and toms and then filling in just what you need with the overheads can be the best plan. Whether you're using either approach, here are some very important considerations:

1. Mic type: Cymbals produce a strong transient when struck with a drumstick. To capture the most accurate version of the cymbal transients and the complexity of the overall kit, condenser mics are the most common choice. For a warmer, fuller sound, some engineers prefer to use high-quality ribbon mics for overheads.

2. Stereo overhead mic position: There are four commonly used stereo overhead configurations, 1) spaced overheads are common in a live sound setting where isolation is the primary consideration, 2) the X-Y configuration is popular in a studio where it's most important that the overheads are phase coherent, 3) the ORTF configuration, similar to the X-Y but spread apart slightly, is still phase coherent but with a little wider sound, and 4) spaced overheads that are equidistant from the snare drum.

			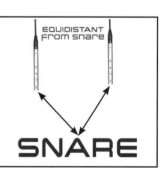
The X-Y hangs roughly over the center of the kit and captures an accurate stereo image. Because the mic capsules are on the same plane and very close together, this provides an image that is phase coherent and sounds good when combined to mono.	*Like the X-Y, the ORTF hangs roughly over the center of the kit from two or three feet above the drummer's head. This technique provides a wider image of the kit but still collapses well to mono.*	*The spaced pair doesn't sum to mono well without quite a bit of experimentation. In the studio, this isn't the best technique. In a live application, it can help improve isolation and it isn't problematic through a stereo system.*	*Even though these mics aren't on the same plane, they are equidistant from the snare drum. Therefore, in stereo, the image is wide and full, but the snare drum is phase-coherent at the center position.*

3. Mono Overhead Mic Positions: Stereo overheads provide a wide and natural drumset image, but especially when using close mics on the kick, snare, and toms, a mono overhead has perfect phase coherence and can do an excellent job blending the cymbals into the kit sound. Position the mic over the kit in line with the drummer's head. Move the mic up and down to find the best balance.

4. Pads: Even though overheads are two or three feet above the kit, drums are loud, so it's advisable to apply the on-board mic **pads**. If the mic overdrives at all, the transients will be dulled, robbing life and expression from the drums.

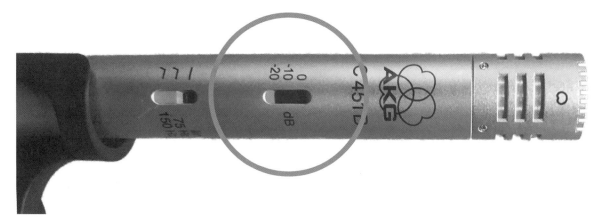

It's important to apply the -10 or -20 dB pad when using condenser mics to capture overheads and hi-hats. Listen to each setting and use the one that sounds the cleanest and most distortion-free.

5. Hi-hat mic type: The hi-hats produce extreme transients. Therefore, condenser microphones are the typical choice, and it's important to apply the microphone's on-board pad.

6. Hi-hat mic position: For a bright and tight sound, aim the mic toward the bell of the top hi-hat. For a dark, sloshy hi-hat sound, aim the mic toward the outer edge of the top cymbal. For a warmer, smoother sound, many engineers prefer a ribbon microphone on the hats.

Like any cymbal, the high frequencies are at the bell and the lows are at the outer edge of the cymbal. Move the mic to find the best sound for the music.

> **TIP:** If you can only use two mics on the kit, consider placing them on either side of the drummer's head, level with the ears, and aiming forward. Drummers naturally adjust their playing so the drums are well-balanced to their ears. This technique can capture a very natural drumset sound. It's also an option worth trying for overheads.

TECHNIQUE 16
Drum Room Mics

OVERVIEW: Room mics can add a lot of interest to the drum sound. The close mics combined with the overhead and hi-hat mics typically provide plenty of balance and pan options; however, it usually takes a little extra effort to build a drum sound that has interest and pizzazz. When tracking drums in a large or medium-sized room, set up a couple of mics away from the drums during the initial take. They can add another dimension to the drum sound.

CHALLENGE: The effectiveness of room mics all depends on the room the drums are tracked in, and how the room mics are deployed. Commercial recording studios usually have great-sounding, project-tested recording spaces. That's one of the reasons they continue to have value in the world of audio production. The typical home studio doesn't have any room that's capable of adding a lot more dimension to the drum sound. I'll mention some techniques that can help you get the most out of the home studio, but there is real musical value in at least recording the drum tracks in a commercial studio.

SOLUTION: The reality is that most home recordists either can't afford to regularly rent a commercial studio to record drums, or they'd just rather be able to work out of the comfort of their own home studio. Here are some great ways to incorporate room mics when you're tracking drums at home:

1. Choose the room wisely: When tracking drums, reflections off surfaces close to the drums are problematic because they combine out-of-phase sounds with the direct sounds from the drums, which can quickly cause them to sound hollow and tonally colored. So, if you can only track drums in a small room, such as a bedroom, then room mics aren't necessary. You're better off in that scenario to add simulated room sound with reverberation. Try tracking drums in the largest rooms in your house, often the living room, family room, or garage. A two- or three-car garage can be a good choice for tracking drums because the ceiling is usually open, and there are likely things stored randomly in the rafters, which provides diffusion and bass trapping. Also, any shelves help absorb and randomize reflections. Granted, garages aren't very isolated from outside noises, but drums are loud, and recording is all about capturing a great performance. A few noises from outside aren't likely to destroy your recording.

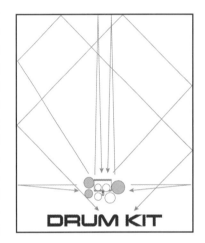

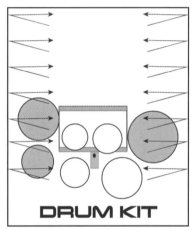

Notice that the reflections from the drumset on the left travel farther around the room so the sound that arrives back at the drum mics adds a larger ambiance. However, the drums on the right are in a small room so the reflections off the surrounding surfaces are strong and nearly instantaneous, causing a problematic phase relationship and an unappealing sound.

2. Mic choice for room mics: Since the drums contain transients and complex waveforms, condenser microphones are the go-to choice for room mics. In particular, large-diaphragm condenser mics are the typical choice because they tend to capture a full and accurate sound.

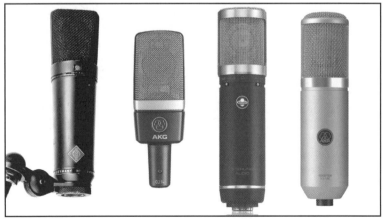

Typically, large-diaphragm condenser mics are used as room mics, although high-quality small-diaphragm mics also provide good results, including accurate transients and the ability to capture fine sonic detail.

3. Aiming the room mics: In a very large room, omnidirectional mics are often used to capture the full impact of the room sound. If the drums are at one end of the room, try placing the room mics two-thirds to three-quarters of the way to the other end, 6 to 8 feet apart, and aiming back at the drums. Experiment with the exact distance—it makes a difference in the sound. Any stereo microphone or stereo mic technique is worth trying for room mics, too. When tracking drums in a medium-sized room, try using cardioid room mics about halfway to the far wall but aimed away from the drum kit. This effectively increases the time it takes for the room sound to get to the mic because it has to bounce off the far wall first, and therefore, can increase the apparent room size.

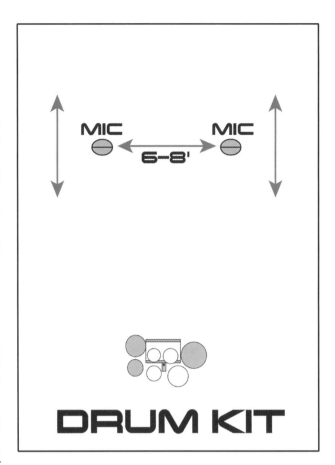

4. Height of the room mics: If the room is large, aim the room mics at the kit roughly level with the drummer's head. It's also common to place the room mics on tall stands about 10 feet in the air. In a large room, try setting a single large-diaphragm mic about 6 inches above the floor and about three-quarters of the way toward the far wall, adjacent to the drums. This mono mic should be positioned carefully to get the right amount of fullness. It can augment the sound, but it's also good for special effects.

5. Using additional mics to make the room sound larger than it is: Once the drums are set up, especially if they're in a smaller room, try adding additional mics in other rooms. Leave the doors open, and the drums will fill up most of the rooms in a house. These mics will dramatically increase the apparent room sound, especially if you place the additional mics in rooms with hard surfaces, such as a kitchen or bathroom.

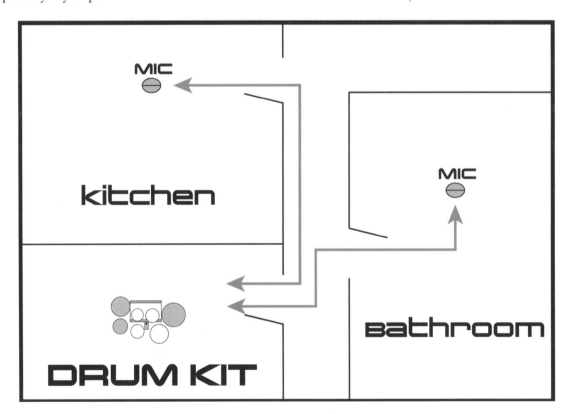

TIP: Compress the room microphones to create a very blended sound that you can add to the overall drum mix. Adding reverberation to the overheads helps increase the apparent room size while maintaining the intimacy of the close mics.

OVERVIEW: When tracking drums in the digital realm, it's usually recommended to save all equalization until mixdown. Since noise isn't really an issue, adding highs, if required for the right sound, doesn't increase the noise level. That's not true in the analog domain. When recording to tape or in live sound, it's important to understand equalization techniques and to apply them to the tape or show.

CHALLENGE: No matter what the circumstance, excessive equalization might solve a problem, but it might also create a problem that's difficult to overcome during mixdown. The best approach to any tracking task is to find the best microphone for the job and to place it so that sound is just what you'll expect to need in the mix. Any radical equalization applied during tracking is only based on speculation—the mix might require a completely different approach once it comes together.

SOLUTION: During tracking, it's almost always best to apply minimal EQ, saving room for changes during mixdown. Here are a few recommended equalization techniques for drums.

1. Kick Drum: Close-miked drums tend to include excessive lower midrange frequencies between about 300 and 600 Hz, creating a sound as if there's a blanket over the kick drum track. We could turn up the highs around 3 or 4 kHz to clean up the sound and the lows below 100 Hz to round them out, but that's not the best way to start. To uncover the highs and lows, turn down the low midrange band. That will clean up the sound dramatically. If you still want to add some highs to accentuate the attack and some lows to fill out the sound, then you'll only need 1, 2, or 3 dB boost instead of several dB. Here is a typical bass drum EQ curve:

Typical kick drum EQ

2. Snare Drum: Even though the snare drum is close-miked, it doesn't tend to have the thickness that close-miked kick and toms do, especially if the mic is aimed at the spot where the stick hits the snare head. It usually benefits from a boost of a few dB between 5 and 8 kHz. It can also sometimes benefit from a boost around 500 or 600 Hz with the lows below 150 Hz being rolled off with a high-pass filter.

Typical snare drum EQ

3. Toms: The way the toms are miked makes a big difference in the sound. Aiming the mics where the stick hits the head helps accentuate the attack, and if there's room to keep the mics 5 or 6 inches above the head, then that helps clean up the sound, too. However, the mics often need to be a little closer to the toms to increase isolation and to stay out of the way of the drummer's sticks. Either way, close-miking a tom tends to result in an overabundance in the low midrange band between about 300 and 600 Hz. Below is a typical tom EQ curve.

4. Overheads: When relying heavily on the overheads for the fullness of the drumset sound, it's a good idea to bypass the EQ and move the mics to find the best sound. But, when using the close mics to capture the drums, try using a high-pass filter to eliminate the lowest frequencies below about 250 Hz. To brighten the sound of the cymbals, apply a shelving EQ starting at about 8 or 10 kHz. It is preferable to apply the same equalization to both mics when using stereo overheads.

Typical tom EQ

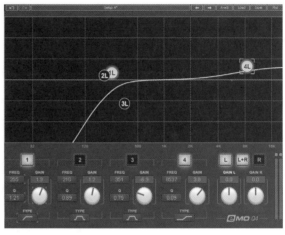

Typical overhead EQ

5. Hi-Hat: There's a wide range of acceptable hi-hat sounds, ranging from a crisp and tight sound, where an EQ similar to a typical overhead is appropriate, to a little more dark and trashy sound, where a cut below about 100 Hz along with a slight boost between 800 and 1000 Hz is appropriate.

6. Room Mics: There are many possibilities for the equalization of the room mics. Everything depends on the sound of the room and what the drum sound needs in order to be best-suited to the overall mix. It's a good idea to start blending the room mics into the mix using a flat EQ. Then, if a certain range needs to be boosted or cut, the EQ can be customized for the production.

Typical hi-hat EQ for a darker tone

Start with the EQ flat for the room mics, then make adjustments to suit the overall sound

> **TIP:** Always get the best sounds you can using mic choice and technique before adding EQ so that you use the least amount of EQ to find the sound you need. However, don't be shy about applying the amount of EQ required to find the best sound for the music. For example, often a deep cut in the low midrange is needed to open up the sound of the toms or the kick drum. That's acceptable if the sound is right.

TECHNIQUE 18
One Mic on Drums

OVERVIEW: Most of the time, close-miking the drumset is preferred. But, sometimes miking the kit with a minimal mic setup is necessary, either due to a lack of channels, lack of microphones, or a desire for a simpler, more organic drum sound. There's nothing wrong with using fewer mics to track drums. In fact, it is a preferred way to track drums in some genres. A lot of great music has been recorded using a single mic on the drumset, especially prior to the modern era—tracks are now virtually limitless.

CHALLENGE: Using fewer mics on the drums forces us to make balance and tone decisions during tracking because there is limited ability to make those changes during mixdown. Finding the best balance of the complete drumset takes some experimentation, by moving the mic(s) a bit this way and that, but it is possible. When listening to the drummer play, stand in front of the kit and then move around until everything sounds balanced. The drummer hears everything in the perfect balance when he or she is playing the drums, so setting a mic just above the drummer's head might work well. The location where the drums are perfectly balanced changes depending on the type of drum part and especially on the way the drummer plays the kit. Tracking drums with one mic can be very effective if you find the best position for the mic and process the track effectively during mixdown. Start with a few ideas about what might work, and then fine-tune the mic positions until you find the sound that best suits the music.

SOLUTION: The following techniques provide a good starting point for discovering usable drum sounds:

1. One mic in front of the kit: Start by standing in front of the drums while the drummer plays. Move your head around until you find a spot that has a good balance of the drums and cymbals. Set the mic at that position, and then record the drummer playing grooves, fills, and crashes. One mic doesn't capture the stereo image that the human ear does, so it might take some experimentation to find the location that captures the best sound. Move the mic from low to high along an arc in front of the kit to locate the desired balance of drums and cymbals.

2. A single microphone positioned above the drumset is sometimes a good choice with its effectiveness dependent on the kind of music being tracked and how loud the drummer plays: For a light jazz or pop song, simply adjust the position of the mic forward to back or side to side to find the best balance of the drums and cymbals. For a song that demands a very aggressive drummer using a lot of crashes, rides, and crash rides, a single mic over the kick will typically capture the cymbals much louder than the drums.

3. Position a single mic above the drummer's head aiming forward: Since drummers intuitively adjust their playing for a musical balance, a microphone at this location should capture a musical balance of the kit. Slight adjustments to the mic up and down or front to back should produce a well-balanced blend of the drums and cymbals. However, the mic should remain directly over the drummer's head.

TIP: To increase the apparent size of the room that the drums are recorded in, set up a cardioid mic in front of the drums, but aim the mic away from the drumset toward the far wall. This increases the distance from the drums to the mic capsule because the mic captures the reflection from the far wall.

TECHNIQUE 19
Two Mics on Drums

OVERVIEW: Using two mics to capture the sound of the drumset more than doubles the possibilities. It's effective to use any of the stereo mic techniques in front of or around the kit. Another possiblility includes using one of the mics to close-mike the kick or the snare and the other to fill in the balance of the kit for a mono technique that still enjoys the power of a close-miked kick or snare.

CHALLENGE: Like the single-mic techniques, two-mic techniques on the kit depend on finding the best location for a perfect balance of the drums and cymbals. The exact location is very specific to the song, drums, drummer, and type of groove. Some drummers have a heavy hi-hat hand while others have a tastefully light touch on all the drums. If the groove is centered around the toms, a completely different location is demanded compared to a light Latin groove. When tracking several songs, assess the drum balance with each new song to make sure the kit fits.

SOLUTION: The following two-mic techniques provide a good starting point for discovering very usable drum sounds:

1. This double mic technique uses a single dynamic mic on the kick drum (Shure Beta 52 pictured) along with a single condenser mic aiming down at the kit (AKG 451 B pictured). The kick mic provides good control over the kick drum's sound and balance. Experiment by moving the mic in front of the hole—or just in front of the head if there isn't a hole—or by positioning the mic inside the kick. Adjust the mic above the kit up and down and front to back to locate the position that records the best balance of the kit.

2. Placing two condenser mics above the kit in an X-Y configuration captures a musical balance and a solid stereo image. Move the mics up and down and/or front to back to locate the position that captures the most musical balance.

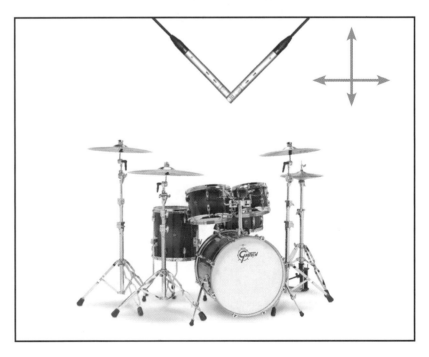

3. Position one microphone on either side of the drummer's head, level with his or her ears and aiming forward. The drummer adjusts his or her playing for a good musical balance, so two mics positioned close to the ears captures this and a solid stereo image.

4. This technique uses a bidirectional ribbon mic to capture the toms, snare, and cymbals with a dynamic mic on the kick drum. The figure-8 pattern of the top mic uses the nulls at 90- and 270-degrees off-axis to minimize the cymbals and capture a better balance of the overall kit. On the kick, there is a dynamic cardioid mic positioned near the top of the kick drum from a distance of about six inches and aimed down at the front head. This technique was used on several of the early Beatles recordings.

TIP: Once you find the best drum sound for your music using one or two mics, try inserting a compressor or peak limiter in the signal path. Adding a dynamics processor helps blend the drums and brings them forward in the mix.

TECHNIQUE 20
Three Mics on Drums

OVERVIEW: Using three or four mics to capture the drumset offers several very useful options. For almost all popular genres, the kick and snare sounds define the musical relevance of the overall drum sound. With most three- and four-mic techniques, at least one of those microphones will be used on the kick drum, and many will use the second mic to capture the snare drum. Techniques using three microphones on drums are useful and greatly expand the sound compared to using two mics. Two of the three mics can capture a solid stereo image of the kit, and the third mic can add punch or intimacy in close proximity to the kick or snare.

CHALLENGE: Finding the perfect balance is often difficult when using a limited number of microphones. When close-miking a kit, many times we have the luxury of setting up one or two pairs of room mics and possibly a mono mic in front of the kit down close to the floor. This provides more options than we might need during mixdown. With a minimal setup, we need to find the proper musical balance during tracking because, if the drum balances aren't right, then the only way to repair the problem is to re-track the drums—a real problem for a session in which the band played live together because there's probably a lot of leakage from the original drums on the other mics.

SOLUTION: Choosing the best placement for any minimal mic setup is of primary importance. When chosen and positioned wisely, three mics can capture a very usable drum sound. There are quite a few effective ways to utilize three mics to record a drumset, but the following will provide a starting point for dreaming up other possibilities.

1. One kick mic with two overheads in an X-Y configuration: This configuration provides a close-miked kick drum along with a stable stereo X-Y configuration that collapses reliably to mono. Experiment with the position of the X-Y mics to find the best blend and balance of drums and cymbals.

2. One kick, one, snare, and one overhead: Although this three-mic technique sacrifices a stereo image from the overheads, it adds a close-miked snare, which for some genres is almost as important as the close-miked kick drum.

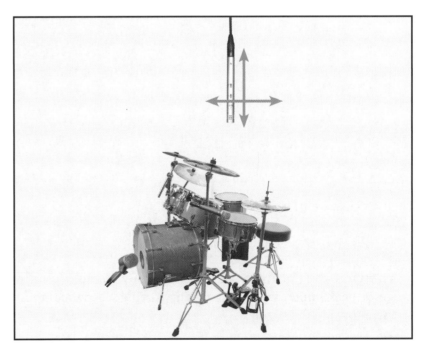

3. One kick and two overheads in an equidistant configuration: Place one of the mics in front of or inside the kick drum. Use the other two mics as overheads making sure that both remain equidistant from the snare drum to maintain a solid phase relationship. Position one of the mics a few feet over the snare drum pointing straight down. Measure the distance from the snare's top head to the mic above it. Make sure that the mic over the floor tom is exactly the same distance from the snare as the snare overhead mic. The other mic can be positioned anywhere on the arc along the floor-tom side; just make sure it's the same distance from the snare.

TIP: With a minimal mic setup, start with the overhead(s) to find a good balance and full, warm tone. Work to get the toms full and clean. With the overall balance established, use the close mic to add intimacy and power.

TECHNIQUE 21
Four Mics on Drums

OVERVIEW: Using four mics to capture the drumset offers several useful options. For almost all popular genres, the kick and snare sounds define the musical relevance of the overall drum sound. With these four-mic techniques, one of those microphones will be used on the kick drum, and the second mic is used to capture the snare drum. The other two mics are used to capture a balance of the toms and cymbals, but the kick and snare sounds can be finely tuned to fit the genre.

CHALLENGE: Close-miking the drums is the preferred way to track drums. However, in many applications, an appropriate drum sound can be captured with fewer mics. The room that the drums are in impacts the sound more when tracking with three or four mics than when close-miking. This is because the mics need to be farther away from the kit in order to capture a balanced blend of drums and cymbals.

SOLUTION: Choosing the best placement for any minimal mic setup is of primary importance. Four mics can capture a very usable drum sound. In fact, for jazz recordings along with some folk and country styles, the blended sound of a four-mic approach is preferable. There are quite a few effective ways to utilize four mics to record a drumset. The following will provide a start for dreaming up other possibilities.

1. One kick, one snare, and two overheads in an X-Y configuration: This four-mic technique uses a kick mic, snare mic, and X-Y overheads. Gaining close-miked control over both the kick and snare is very useful and the X-Y configuration provides a solid stereo image that collapses reliably to mono.

2. One kick, one snare, and two overheads in an equidistant configuration: The close-miked kick and snare add a solid punch to any groove. The two overheads are positioned so they're equidistant from the snare, providing an excellent balance on the rest of the kit and maintaining a reliable phase relationship when the drums are summed to mono.

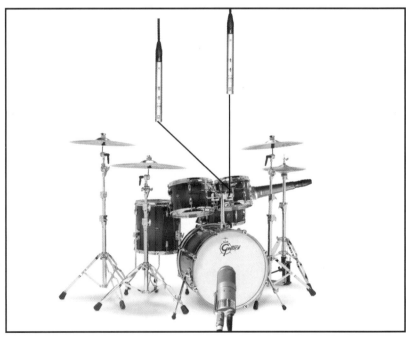

3. One kick, one snare, one above the rack tom(s), and one above the floor tom(s): This technique is similar to a close-miking technique because it uses a kick mic, snare mic, and two overheads that are positioned over the rack tom(s) and floor tom(s), leaving enough distance to capture the cymbals. Move the overheads up and down over the toms to find the location that captures a full, powerful sound that is balanced well with the cymbals.

4. One kick, one snare, one mic facing forward near the drummers left ear, and one mic facing forward near the drummer's right ear: With this setup, a natural sound is captured that includes a powerful kick and snare along with a tom and cymbal image that matches the drummer's perspective. Be sure to monitor these drums in mono at some point. If the sound is hollow and weak, then invert the polarity on both of the overheads. If the sound is more full and powerful with the overhead polarities reversed, then you can be sure that it's safe to switch back to monitoring in stereo.

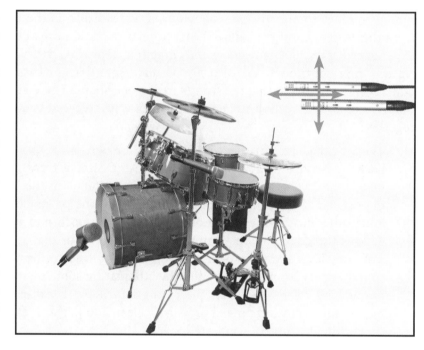

TIP: Experiment and be creative. Try anything that you can dream up just to see if it produces great results or if it's simply part of the process of learning what works and what doesn't. The techniques that I've mentioned are tested, but always listen to the music and imagine what type of customized sound might work best with the production.

TECHNIQUE 22
Bass Guitar DI

OVERVIEW: The bass guitar sound is a very important part of a great mix. Many bassists carry a bass amp along with them to every gig because they love the sound their bass creates through the amp. However, the best approach to capturing the bass guitar in the studio—or live for that matter—is often through the use of a direct box, also referred to as a DI (direct input). The purpose of the DI is to receive the high-impedance instrument-level signal from the bass and transform it so that it can be connected to the low-impedance mic-level input on a mixing console.

CHALLENGE: When the bassist shows up at a gig with a bass amp and speaker cabinet, he or she should remain flexible and work with the sound engineer to discover the best plan. Very large venues have enough airspace to absorb bass and guitar amplifiers without too muchof a problem, but in a small venue, the bass amp can quickly dominate the mix without the bassist even realizing it. In the studio, the sound that comes from the cabinet may or may not work well in the mix. When tracking bass guitar, it's fundamentally important to make sure there are enough options for the bass sound once it's time for mixdown.

SOLUTION: For each tracking session, always have a DI set up and ready for the bassist to plug into. It's always worth running the bass through a DI and connecting it to a recorder track. That doesn't mean that it's not a good idea to mic the bass cabinet or, if it's available on the amp head, to connect the line-level output from the head to another channel. It never hurts to track more options than you might need to use, but most experienced tracking engineers would agree that capturing the bass guitar through a DI to a separate DAW track is the right thing to do. Also, always make sure that the bass guitar is set up so that it plays in tune up and down the neck and that the strings are in good shape. There are several different types of direct boxes and a number of ways to connect everything together.

1. Tracking the bass with a passive DI: There are two basic types of direct boxes: **passive** and **active**. Passive DIs use a simple transformer to match the level and **impedance** of the bass guitar with the level and impedance of the console input. The quality of the passive DI makes a big difference in the sound of the bass. The transformer in the DI defines the quality of the sound and the integrity of the conversion from one level and type to another. Low-quality transformers can rob sound quality from the bass guitar by attenuating some high and low frequencies. Many engineers prefer the Radial JDI because it has a high-quality transformer and provides a clean and faithful representation of the instrument connected to it.

2. Tracking the bass with an active DI: Active direct boxes contain powered electronic circuits designed to bring back the highs and lows that are diminished in the passive DI. When comparing similar quality passive and active DIs, it's easy to hear that the active DI provides a sound that is stronger overall, but it's also clearer in the high frequencies and fuller in the low frequencies. Active DIs require power from batteries or from the 48-volt **phantom power** supplied by the console. It's often held that it is best to use an active DI for a passive bass guitar or a passive DI for an active bass guitar. However, it's always best to try both to hear the differences and decide which sound is best for the music. Especially when considering active DIs, it would be a mistake not to mention that, although there are a lot of really great options, many of them are quite expensive. Radial DIs fall into a mid-price point, but try out anything from Avalon, REDDI, Rupert Neve Design, BAE, Countryman, or Telefunken.

3. Tracking the bass with a tube DI: A typical active DI uses phantom power to run its internal solid-state circuits. A tube DI, like the Radial Firefly, is an active DI that uses power to run its tube-based circuitry. A tube DI usually uses 120-volt AC power to run its electronic circuits, which is slightly less convenient than the phantom power solid-state active DIs. However, a tube DI typically makes the source sound warmer, fuller, and more pleasing to the ear.

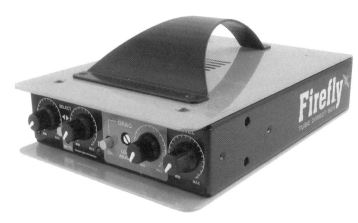

4. Tracking the bass with a DI and a mic on the bass cabinet: Every DI includes an instrument input and a 1/4-inch thru output that is used to pass the signal along to an amplifier input. If the bassist shows up with an amplifier, simply plug the bass into the DI and the XLR output from the DI to the console XLR input. Then connect the thru jack to the amplifier input using a regular guitar cable. Use a microphone to record the sound of the bass cabinet to its own track with the DI output recording to another track. Blend the sounds during mixdown.

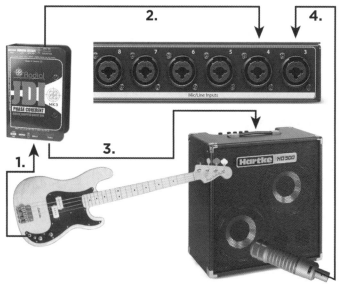

1. Bass to DI input *2. DI XLR output to mixer/interface XLR input* *3. DI thru jack to bass amp input* *4. Microphone on speaker cabinet to mixer/interface XLR input*

5. Tracking the bass with a DI and the line-level output from the bass amplifier: In addition to the speaker output, some amplifier heads provide a balanced output that's ready to plug into the console channel. Connect the XLR output to its own channel. Record the amp output and the DI output to separate channels, and since the bass cabinet is there, mic it and send it to another separate track. With three options to choose from during mixdown, you should be able to find a great bass sound that fits the music well. The bass sound that is heard on most commercial recordings is recorded straight from the bass through a direct box. Therefore, you might discover that, even though you have recorded some options, the DI signal is the one that establishes the most solid foundation for the music.

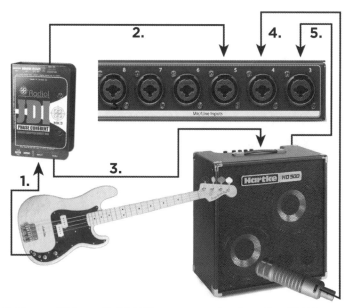

1. Bass to DI input *2. DI XLR output to mixer/interface XLR input* *3. DI thru jack to bass amp input* *4. Microphone on speaker cabinet to mixer/interface XLR input* *5. Amp line-level output to mixer/interface*

TIP: It takes a long time for bass guitar strings to wear out, but if the bassist has oily skin or if climate conditions cause dirt and grime to stick to the strings, then they might begin to sound lifeless and dull. To bring life back to your dirty bass strings, boil them in water for 10 to 15 minutes, dry them off, and put them back on the bass. Chances are they'll sound as good as new!

TECHNIQUE 23
Miking the Bass Cabinet

OVERVIEW: Tracking the bass guitar through a DI is always worth doing because it doesn't exclude any other options. Since the DI has a thru jack that can be connected to the amplifier input, it's a pretty simple matter to record a DI, a miked speaker cabinet, and a direct output from the amplifier at the same time. But, make sure to record all of those options to separate tracks so that the sound can be customized for mixdown. Although it's worth recording the bass from a DI, there are certain amp and speaker combinations that are magical, adding a personality that surpasses anything a DI can deliver. If there is a bass rig, put a mic in front of the cabinet and track it.

CHALLENGE: Capturing the full sound of the bass cabinet can be a challenge. For example, the standard speaker cabinet for the highly touted Ampeg SVT contains eight 10-inch speakers. The sound is incredible from a few feet away because the 80 inches of total speaker move a lot of air and sound fantastic. However, in a session or a live gig, leakage might be an issue. This calls for close miking, and a single mic on one 10-inch speaker doesn't get the same effect. However, a more standard configuration for a bass rig uses a single 15-inch speaker, which is the perfect setup for close miking.

SOLUTION: Assess each unique situation with an open mind. If it's possible to isolate the bass cabinet, then it will be much easier to get a great sound because the mics can be set back a little farther. The recurring theme for getting excellent recordings is to choose the best mic for the job and put it in the location that captures the best sound from the source. That's definitely the case when miking a bass speaker cabinet.

1. Dynamic Microphones: Dynamic microphones are the most commonly used mic type for recording a bass guitar speaker cabinet. They can handle high volume levels without breaking up, and they are designed to be used in close proximity to the source. The best dynamic mic for the job depends on the sound and volume being produced by the amplifier. Microphones designed for kick drum are usually a good choice for miking the bass cabinet, including the Shure Beta 52, AKG D-110, Audix D6, and Electro-Voice RE20. However, mics like the Shure SM57, Sennheiser 421, and Shure Beta 57 are also good choices.

2. Ribbon Microphones: Ribbon microphones capture a richer, warmer tone from the bass cabinet. The appropriate choice of a ribbon mic depends completely on the sound that's coming from the cabinet. If the bass sound is aggressive and/or distorted, the ribbon mic will capture a sound that blends well with the rest of the mix. The Royer R-122 MkII is a great choice for bass because it has both a pad to address extreme volume and a high-pass filter to compensate for the proximity effect with the mic close to the speaker. When using a ribbon mic on a speaker, angle the mic down slightly so the air from the speaker isn't blowing straight into the ribbon element, which can damage the ribbon.

SPEAKER CABINET (SIDE)

3. Condenser Microphones: Condenser microphones aren't the typical choice for miking the bass cabinet because the loud bass can overdrive the mic capsule. Also, condensers aren't typically used because the bass guitar sound doesn't contain many transients or frequencies that extend much past the midrange band. If the bass sound is complex with a broad frequency range, a large-diaphragm condenser mic with a pad and high-pass filter, such as an Audio-Technica 4047 MP, Shure KSM44, or Neumann U 87, should perform well.

4. Position on the speaker: Always keep in mind that, when placing a mic on a speaker, the highs come from the center of the speaker and the lows come from the outer edge of the speaker. Start with the mic facing the center of the speaker's dust cover, and then move the mic toward the outer edge of the speaker while the bassist plays. There will likely be a location where the bass sound is just right.

5. Miking a multi-speaker cabinet: When a bass cabinet contains multiple speakers, especially speakers of differing sizes, place a microphone a few feet away from the cabinet to capture the full sound. Of course, this won't work if several instruments are tracking at once in the same space, but if the cabinet is isolated, listen to the amp while the bassist plays. You should be able to find a spot where the balance and tone are acceptable. Start with the mic at that location and then have a helper move the mic around while you listen to it in the control room. Once you find the best-sounding location for the mic, mark the mic stand and speaker enclosure locations on the floor with gaffer tape to make it easier to reestablish the bass sound if the session needs to be reset.

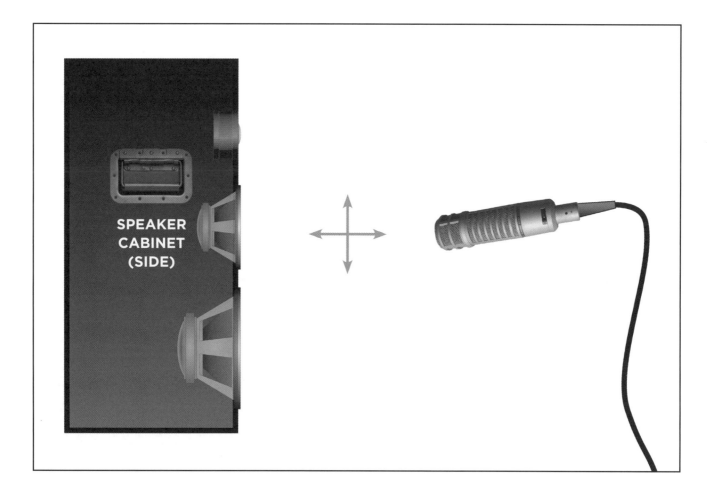

TIP: When combining a direct bass signal with a miked bass cabinet, always zoom in on both waveforms to check their phase relationship. Simply because of the distance between the microphone and the cabinet, the miked signal might be lagging behind the DI signal, which can cause a hollow and weak sound. Nudge the miked signal forward a few samples at a time so it lines up perfectly with the DI signal.

TECHNIQUE 24
Acoustic Guitar

OVERVIEW: The acoustic guitar sound is rich, full of transients, and interesting. There are many variables surrounding the acoustic, and they all have an impact on the recorded sound. Capturing the perfect sound for the music involves an informed use of mics and mic technique. However, a lot of the influence on the sound happens before the guitarist starts playing.

CHALLENGE: The type of musical production is what determines the perfect acoustic guitar sound. During tracking, the producer is the one who should have the big picture in mind and is the one who should make the call about any of the recorded sounds. The physical size of the acoustic guitar makes a big difference in the way the sound sits in the mix. A large- or jumbo-body guitar sound might be too massive for some mixes where a small-body acoustic sound might work perfectly.

SOLUTION: When tracking acoustic guitar, there isn't always an opportunity to switch from a large-body to a small-body guitar. Over time, pay attention to the difference in the sounds of different acoustic guitars. Learn what they sound like and experiment with mic techniques so you can be ready to capture great acoustic guitar tracks.

1. Strings: The acoustic guitar sound depends on having new or relatively new strings. If a guitarist shows up with dirty, dull-sounding guitar strings, it will be difficult getting a great sound, and it shows that the guitarist doesn't understand the recording process. If there is a legitimate reason that the music needs the sound of an acoustic with gunked up dirty strings, then that's what needs  to happen. However, as a rule, the acoustic should be strung with strings that produce a wide frequency band and clear, clean transients. Dulling the tone of the guitar is simple with equalization, but it's next to impossible to make dull strings sound alive, clear, and clean. The gauge of string also impacts the sound dramatically. A light gauge set of strings typically sounds weak in the lows with a pronounced transient and ample high frequencies. Medium and heavy strings produce a very balanced tone throughout the frequency range with a solid, stable low band and a smooth, clear high band.

2. Neck adjustments: If the guitar neck is bowed and twisted, the nut and bridge need work, and/or the frets are uneven, capturing a great-sounding acoustic guitar track is unlikely. If the guitar has a lot of buzzes and string noises and the notes are in-tune in one position but out-of-tune in another, either save the day (if you're an excellent guitar tech), or do the project a favor and cancel the session until a suitable guitar can be found. It's okay to struggle through some problems, but some things are too detrimental to a production to tolerate.

3. Picks: Most accomplished acoustic guitarists realize that the weight and size of the guitar pick makes a big difference in the sound of the guitar performance. A thin pick produces a sound with more transient as the pick bending and striking the strings provides an exaggerated attack. A thick pick produces a sound that is more solid in the low end without the pronounced transient. The sound produced with a medium pick is still solid in the low band with a clean and stable high-frequency transient.

4. Tunings: Acoustic guitarists go to great lengths to include open strings along with fretted notes because the sound of open strings droning keeps the harmonic and melodic momentum while the guitar sound remains rich and interesting. Alternate tunings and capos are frequently used to take advantage of the rich sound of open strings. The guitarist needs to do a lot of adjusting and compensating for re-tuning, but altered tunings help shape a part that's interesting, unique (because it probably can't be performed on a guitar with traditional tuning), and powerful.

Some popular alternate tunings are **dropped D** tuning (DADGBE), **dropped G** tuning (DGDGBE), **open G** tuning (DGDGBD), **open D** tuning (DADF♯AD), and **DADGAD** (DADGAD).

5. Body size: Guitar bodies come in all sizes, from the jumbo and dreadnought sizes to 3/4- and 1/2-scale guitars and the tiny Papoose guitar. They all sound different. Someone who loves the sound of a jumbo-body acoustic guitar might be underwhelmed with the sound of a small-body guitar. But, the song that needs a small-body sound would not be the same without it.

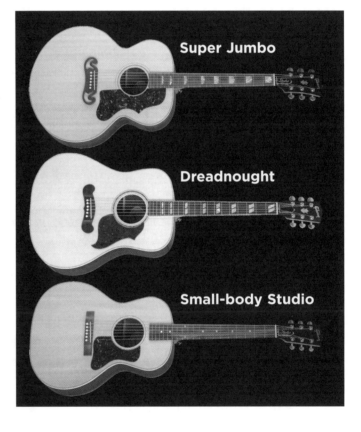

6. Wood: Most acoustic guitars use spruce wood for the guitar top but the sides and back make a big difference in the sound. Rosewood back and sides produce a sound that is clean and clear with strong transients. Guitars that use a soft wood for the sides and back, such as mahogany, produce a sound that is warm and full.

TIP: A high-strung guitar is used frequently in Nashville because it produces a sound that complements the traditional acoustic guitar. It typically uses a standard tuning of EADGBE. The bottom four strings are tuned up one octave. This tuning requires a change of string gauge on the lower strings. Try, from bottom to top: .034, .024, .013, .010, 016, .013.

TECHNIQUE 25
Acoustic Guitar DI

OVERVIEW: An acoustic guitar sounds better when it's tracked using a microphone than when it's tracked using a direct box. Even the best of internal pickup systems can't match the sound of a great mic on a great guitar played by a great guitarist. Also, all internal pickup systems are not created equal. Some are not good, but others are relatively easy on the ears, especially the systems that incorporate a microphone inside the guitar body.

CHALLENGE: The typical internal pickup system for acoustic guitar utilizes a thin ceramic pickup that lays in the bridge saddle underneath the bridge. The pickup runs the length of the bridge from the low strings to the high strings, and the vibrations of the strings are picked up and sent through a preamp to the output jack on the guitar. These systems don't have a particularly warm sound, and most of the time, they provide a signal that sounds a bit brittle, typically with an overabundance of frequencies at about 2 kHz.

SOLUTION: Choosing the right direct box to connect the guitar output to the mixer makes a big difference in the sound of the electric acoustic guitar. Radial makes their JDI passive direct box, which is a very nice DI for acoustic guitar. Depending on the specific guitar, Radial's J48 active DI is also a great choice. Try as many direct boxes as you can on the specific acoustic guitar that you're using. Listen to them all side by side and choose the one that sounds best.

1. DI versus microphone: When using a microphone on an acoustic guitar, there is an incredible degree of flexibility in mic placement and choice. Just make an intelligent mic choice and position the mic for the sound that fits the music. However, when using a DI with the acoustic guitar's on-board pickup system, even though there are often tone controls and possibly a balance control between pickup options, the pickup system is inflexible and almost always sonically inferior to the sound captured from a microphone. But, that doesn't mean that there aren't situations where using a DI is the best choice. When tracking the acoustic guitar in the same room with a band, there might be a prohibitive amount of leakage of the rest of the group into the mic, even if the acoustic guitarist is surrounded by baffles. Like a live show, tracking an acoustic guitar in the same room with the rest of the band makes the use of a direct box the best option.

   If the acoustic guitar has a particularly good electronic pickup system, then record it to a separate track even if the main pickup is from a microphone. There's no harm in recording an extra track, and it might be useful in mixdown.

2. Passive DIs: A passive DI doesn't require power to operate. It uses a transformer to match levels and impedance between the high-impedance instrument output and the mixer's balanced low-impedance XLR input. Since a passive DI doesn't use power, it can't use an electronic circuit to add anything back that the transformer might take from the input signal. Therefore, the transformer quality is fundamentally important to the sound of the instrument through the DI. Compare the sound of several passive DIs to find the best sounding DI for your application. The Radial JDI is an example of a
great-sounding passive DI. It uses a high-quality Jensen transformer.

   Simplicity is the advantage of a passive DI. Since there are no electronic circuits, the passive DI typically produces less noise and distortion and can be very faithful to the sound of the source. When using an active instrument like a keyboard, active bass guitar, or guitar pedal board, passive DIs are typically the best choice. An acoustic guitar that uses a battery is active, so a DI like the JDI is a good choice.

3. Active DIs: Active direct boxes contain electronic circuitry to help compensate for instruments with low-output levels and to restore losses in signal content due to the internal transformer. An active DI can typically receive power either from a battery or from phantom power supplied by the mixing console. The electronic circuit adds a boost in both the lows and highs as well as the overall signal. Although many consider it preferable to use a passive DI with an active acoustic guitar or an active DI with a passive acoustic guitar, it is always best to listen to the available DIs (passive and active) to choose the DI that's best for the music.

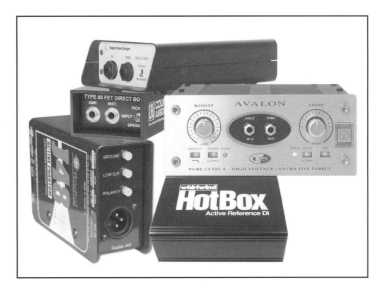

4. Tube DIs: A tube DI is simply an active DI that uses a vacuum-tube-amplifying circuit, unlike a typical active DI that uses a solid-state circuit. The tube circuit helps bring warmth to an acoustic guitar in much the same way that it brings warmth to an electric guitar amplifier. A viable option for acoustic guitar, the tube DI is sometimes a little too warm for a particular guitar, but in some cases, it makes the guitar sound great. Everything depends on the player, strings, guitar part, the pick, and so on.

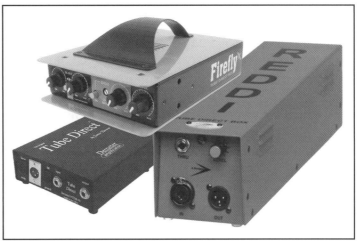

TIP: Record both the miked and DI signals to separate tracks. During mixdown, a blend of the miked and direct signals might be the best sound for the music. However, depending on the production, the miked sound might work best for one part of the song and recording direct might work best for another.

TECHNIQUE 26
Miking Acoustic Guitar

OVERVIEW: Acoustic guitars sound best when miked with a great microphone from the best location for the desired sound. Mics have the ability to capture a full tone with precise and clean transients that can't be rivaled by the best of internal pickup systems. Even the very best pickup systems, which can sound quite decent, don't quite match the clear and natural tone that a great condenser or ribbon mic captures when skillfully positioned.

CHALLENGE: There is one area where capturing the acoustic guitar with a mic simply can't compete with an internal pickup system: isolation. If a band is tracking all together live in the studio, leakage of the rest of the band into the acoustic guitar mic overwhelms the guitar sounds, eliminating any possibility of control during mixdown. Other miked instruments, such as electric guitar amps, bass amps, and drums, fare better in a live tracking session because those instruments are loud enough to dominate the air space in front of the microphone.

SOLUTION: If the studio has a suitable isolation room for the acoustic guitar, then that's the best solution during tracking. If isolation isn't available while tracking the entire group, then wait to record the acoustic as an overdub after the basic tracks are completed. If the acoustic guitar is crucial to the song's feel and groove, then track the guitar through the internal pickup system and then add the overdubbed parts later. It's a good idea to baffle the guitar during tracking so the leakage from the acoustic sound is minimized for the other open mics. There are several important considerations when miking acoustic guitar:

1. Room choice: The size, shape, and design of the acoustical space of the tracking room impacts the recorded sound of any instrument. Acoustic guitar is no exception. If the mic is close to the acoustic guitar, then the room sound will have less impact on the recorded track. However, keeping the mic close to the guitar isn't always ideal. In a large room where the reflections off the closest surfaces aren't damaging to the recorded sound, a balanced sound can be captured from a distance of 2 or 3 feet. In smaller rooms, the mic typically needs to be between 6 and 18 inches from the guitar.

2. Pick choice: The thickness of the guitar pick makes a big difference in both the acoustic and recorded sounds. Thinner picks take on a snappy sound as the pick bends and slaps back into place. The sound is lighter and notably less substantial when the guitarist uses a medium or thick pick. As the thickness of the pick increases, the acoustic guitar sound darkens, producing decreased high-frequency content and a reduction in the crisp transient. Most experienced acoustic guitarists carry a pouch with guitar picks of many different thicknesses that are made from different types of materials, ranging from plastic to nylon to felt and even metal.

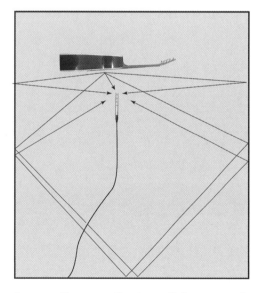

In a small room, reflections off the surrounding surfaces are strong, and they negatively influence the sound at the microphone. Therefore, a distant mic in a small room doesn't produce a warm and appealing tone but rather produces a sound that is harsh and often hollow-sounding.

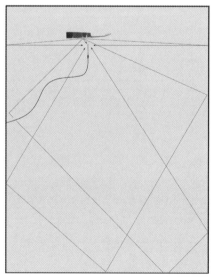

In a large room, reflection from near and far walls take longer to reach the microphone. They lose energy so they aren't destructive to the sound. With baffles and a little bit of isolation, the mic can be farther from the guitar and still produce an excellent sound.

3. Baffles: **Baffles**, also called **gobos** and **screens**, are used to isolate sources being tracked in the same space, absorb unwanted reflections off nearby walls and surfaces, and to keep the source sound from leaking into other open mics in the same acoustical space. Surrounding the acoustic guitar and guitarist with gobos helps tighten the sound when tracking in a large room. Gobos also help shield the guitar sound from close reflections in a small room.

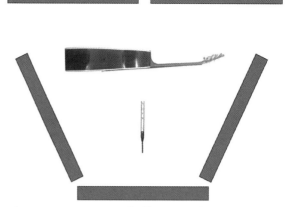

Placing 4' x 4' or 4' x 8' baffles around and behind the guitarist helps minimize reflections and leakage.

4. Mic choice: One of the accepted standards for miking an acoustic guitar is the small-diaphragm condenser mic because they typically have a flat frequency response and pick up a balanced tone, plus they respond very well to transients and waveform detail. This is still true today, but it was especially true in the days of analog tape recorders because it was very important to capture plenty of high-frequency and transient detail. However, when using a modern DAW, we're more interested in capturing an accurate and balanced sound, so ribbon mics have become a popular choice for tracking acoustic guitar. They provide a warm tone and a very natural-sounding transient that is pleasing to the ear and easy to fit into the mix. Large-diaphragm condenser microphones are also a good choice for miking acoustic guitars.

5. Mic position: The mic position, relative to the guitar body, is a crucial factor in capturing the best sound for the music. The typical go-to location for the microphone on an acoustic guitar is in front of the guitar neck about 12 inches above the fretboard, aimed somewhere between the twelfth fret and where the neck joins the body. However, there is a wide range of tone available from the acoustic guitar when the mic is place at different locations. Placing the mic over and behind the bridge captures an abundance of midrange. Positioning the mic over the sound hole captures an abundance of low frequencies while positioning the mic over the fretboard captures an increased amount of high frequencies.

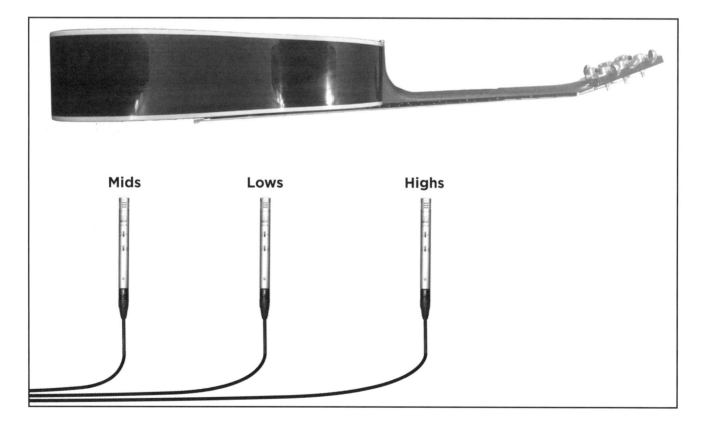

TIP: When in doubt, record multiple tracks of the acoustic guitar. There's no harm in recording two, three, or more mics at a time along with the direct output from the guitar. One of the tracks is likely to work best. Eventually, you'll find the placement you like and won't need to set up so many options.

TECHNIQUE 27
Stereo Miking Acoustic Guitar

OVERVIEW: Using a single (mono) mic is probably the most common approach to tracking acoustic guitar because it's a simple technique, provides for pin-point positioning in the mix, and keeps the acoustic guitar image stable and focused throughout the mix. However, a stereo tracking of the acoustic can quickly add dimension to the mix that wouldn't otherwise exist.

CHALLENGE: Granted, stereo recordings of acoustic guitar sound more impressive when heard in a clean and open production, but in a large-scale production, there isn't typically room in the mix to appreciate the value provided by stereo tracks. When stereo mic techniques are employed, it is very important to confirm that the technique sounds good in stereo and mono.

SOLUTION: The most important decision-making consideration when it comes to whether or not to use stereo miking techniques on acoustic guitar, lies in the scope and needs of the musical production. If the acoustic guitar plays a small part in the musical production, then it's usually best and safest to use a single mic technique. But, if the acoustic plays a starring role in the production, then a stereo recording might be the best approach. With each technique, it's very important to move the mics up and down along the neck to find the best frequency balance and to move the mic from close (6–9 inches) to far away (1–3 feet) until the desired sound is discovered. There are several stereo mic techniques. Here are a few that are tested and proven winners:

1. The X-Y Technique: Anytime a stereo mic technique is appropriate, the X-Y technique is effective and safe. This is called a **coincident** technique because the two mic capsules occupy as close to the same position in space as possible. This technique typically employs two small-diaphragm condenser mics positioned at 90 degrees to each other with one capsule directly over the other, as close together as possible without touching. The X-Y technique also works well with large-diaphragm condenser

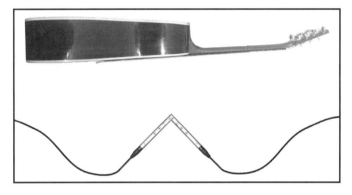

mics. The sound captured by this technique is not an incredibly wide sound, but it definitely sounds stereo and is very focused. With one capsule directly above the other, this configuration is **phase coherent**, meaning that when the two channels are summed to mono—like they would be when the song is played at a gig through a mono sound system—the acoustic sound is still solid and full. When there are phase problems between mics used to capture stereo tracks, they might sound great in stereo, but in mono, the guitar might disappear in the mix or at least sound hollow and weak. The X-Y technique provides a stereo image that's a little bass-heavy from the mic aimed back at the sound hole and a little more focused on the high frequencies from the mic aimed at the neck.

2. The Vertical X-Y Technique: The vertical X-Y is just like the X-Y technique, using two condenser mics forming a 90-degree angle to each other with the capsules as close together as possible without touching. However, unlike the traditional X-Y technique where the two mics are positioned along a horizontal plane, this technique aims the mics relative to the vertical plane. One mic points up at the low notes and the other mic points down at high notes. Therefore, the stereo image is more like

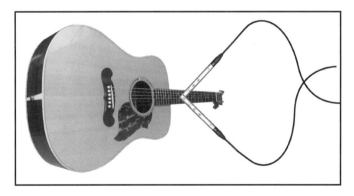

a piano, where the left-to-right balance runs from the low notes to the high notes, unlike like the traditional horizontal X-Y where the stereo balance goes from low frequencies to high frequencies.

3. The ORTF Technique: Even though the ORTF technique doesn't incorporate coincident capsules, it provides a wide stereo image that still sums well to mono when adhering to the specifications of the technique. With this technique, the two microphones are aimed away from each other at a 110-degree angle, and the capsules are to be separated by 17 centimeters (6.69 inches).

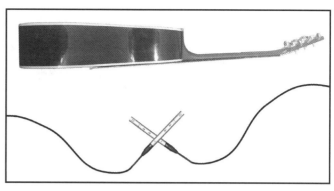

4. The Blumlein Technique: The Blumlein technique uses two bidirectional mics in a configuration that's very similar to the X-Y. The mics are turned 90 degrees apart, and the capsules are on the same plane, positioned as close together as possible without touching. This is a great technique when the studio room sounds great. It is like the X-Y, but there is more room sound because the back sides of the mics are picking up sound. Condenser and ribbon mics are both excellent choices for this technique.

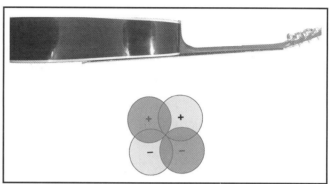

5. The Spaced Pair Technique: This technique is a little risky, but it can provide an excellent stereo sound. Point both mics at the front of the guitar, keeping them parallel to each other. Place one mic between the sound hole and the bridge and the other mic over the fretboard aimed at about the point where the neck joins the guitar body. Experiment with exact mic placement to find a great sound. Remember, it's just as important to monitor the stereo configuration in mono to make sure the sound

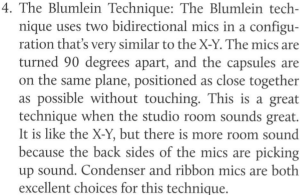

remains hollow and weak, then move the mics slightly closer or farther apart until the mono sound is full and focused. It is then safe to switch back to stereo, and you can trust that the recorded tracks won't be problematic when it's time to mix.

6. The Mid-Side (M-S) Technique: The M-S technique uses two mics—one mic with a cardioid polar pattern and the other mic with a bidirectional pattern—but this technique actually takes up three tracks. The cardioid (mid) mic should be aimed at the acoustic guitar as if that were the only mic in the setup. That way, it captures the best possible full-range balanced tone. The bidirectional (side) mic should be positioned with the side (90-degrees off-axis) aimed at the same point on the guitar as the

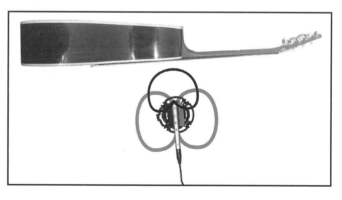

cardioid mic and with the capsule directly above or below the cardioid capsule. In the mix, the side mic is panned hard to one side, duplicated in the DAW with an inverted polarity and panned hard to the other side. This makes the two side channels 180 degrees out of phase, which provides a wide stereo image. However, when summed to mono, the two side channels completely cancel each other, and all that's left is the center mic.

TIP: In our current DAW era, ribbon microphones have become a very viable option for acoustic guitar. Tracking with ribbon mics captures a very natural, smooth sound that fits well in the mix. If the technique requires a cardioid mic, then try the Beyer M160, a fantastic-sounding cardioid ribbon mic.

TECHNIQUE 28
Miking the Electric Guitar Cabinet

OVERVIEW: The term "electric guitar" doesn't say too much about the actual sounds created by the modern electric guitarist. In many genres, this is an era of layered effects with long reverb decay times and long repeating delays that nearly obscure the source guitar tone. Still, in some genres we hear more down-to-earth tones that rely on the characteristic electric guitar tone. Anyone involved in recording music should at least recognize the characteristic sound differences between the most popular electric guitars—Les Paul, Stratocaster, Telecaster, and semi hollow and hollow body guitars. Understanding these differences will guide the tracking engineer through techniques that will capture the intended essence of the guitar sounds.

CHALLENGE: Techniques for miking the speaker(s) in the cabinet impact the recorded sound. That's why it's important to be familiar with traditional guitars and the sounds they deliver. Mic choice and position can radically influence the miked sound, so it's important to be informed about traditional sounds while working closely with the guitarist and/or producer to customize the sound to fit the music.

SOLUTION: Each microphone type offers a relatively predictable result when positioned in front of a speaker in the guitarist's speaker cabinet. In addition, the microphone position in relation to the speaker is crucial in shaping the recorded sound. The following considerations impact recorded electric guitar sounds:

1. Mic choice: Dynamic microphones are the most popular choice for miking the electric guitar speaker cabinet. Specifically, the Shure SM57 has been the go-to mic for tracking electric guitar pretty much since its release in 1965. The SM57 is amply able to withstand the high sound pressure level delivered by a guitar amp, and it has a high-end presence peak that accentuates the clarity range of the guitar along with a roll-off in the low end that makes it a good choice for close-miking. Most dynamic mics, such as the Sennheiser 421, Electro-Voice RE20, and Blue Encore 100/200 produce similar results to the SM57, but the combination of its sound quality, affordability, and durability help keep the SM57 at the top of the list of most popular microphones.

   Since the birth of the modern DAW, ribbon microphones have gained an ever-increasing popularity, especially for recording electric guitar. Whereas the SM57's presence peak was useful in the analog era because it helped get more highs to tape, the analog process warmed the tone and helped take the abrasive edge off the recorded guitar sound. DAW playback, on the other hand, is very faithful to the recorded sound. Ribbon microphones capture a warmer and smoother tone than the typical dynamic microphone—a warm tone not too dissimilar to the sound of analog tape. That's why, when Royer introduced the R-121 ribbon mic in 1998, it was instantly embraced by great engineers around the world as an excellent choice for a wide range of recording applications, especially for miking the speakers in a guitar amplifier. On the guitar amp, a ribbon microphone smooths out the abrasive tone that is sometimes captured by a dynamic mic and creates a tone that is easy on the ear and blends very well in mixdown. The Royer R-121, R-122, and the Audio-Technica AT4080 are all excellent choices for miking the electric guitar.

   Condenser mics aren't typically chosen for electric guitar because they are more prone to being overdriven by loud volume. Also, the ability to capture high-frequency detail and accurate transients is a bit wasted on the typical electric guitar sound, which doesn't contain much of either.

2. Attenuation: With a guitar amplifier turned up loud enough to get an aggressive tone, the sound coming from the speaker is extremely loud—loud enough to overdrive the ribbon or condenser capsule. That's why built-in pads are important when recording electric guitar. Condenser microphones aren't as commonly used for electric guitar as dynamic and ribbon mics, but when they're used, it's almost always best to use the built-in pad. Dynamic and ribbon mics can handle loud volume without overdriving the capsule. However, newer active ribbon mics like the Royer R-122 MKII contain built-in amplifying circuitry that can be overdriven by a very loud guitar amp, so the R-122 contains a built-in -12 dB pad.

3. Filters: Due to the proximity effect, full-range condenser and ribbon mics will likely capture a sound that's excessively boomy and bass-heavy when positioned close to the speaker. Most condenser mics contain a built-in high-pass filter (**HPF**) that rolls off the lows. The cut-off frequency for the filter varies from mic to mic, but most high-pass filters roll off the lows somewhere between 40 Hz and 160 Hz. The AKG 414 XLII has built-in high-pass filters at 40, 80, and 160 Hz. Most ribbon mics are passive, so they don't contain filters. However, the active Royer R-122 MKII includes a built-in HPF that rolls off below 100 Hz. Most dynamic mics roll off in the low end already, so there's no HPF required.

Royer R-122 MKII

4. Aiming the mic: The way the microphone is aimed at the speaker makes a very big difference in the captured sound. The cone goes down toward the center of the speaker where the dust cover protects the moving-coil capsule. Aiming the mic at the center of the dust cover captures the most highs. When tracking certain guitar sounds, aiming the mic at the center of the dust cover captures too many highs, resulting in a sound that's very brittle- and harsh-sounding. The warmest sound is found by aiming the mic at the outer edge of the cone. Mic position is also dependent on mic choice. Whereas a dynamic mic might be unduly harsh when aimed at the center of the dust cover, a ribbon mic aimed at that exact same spot might yield the perfect sound.

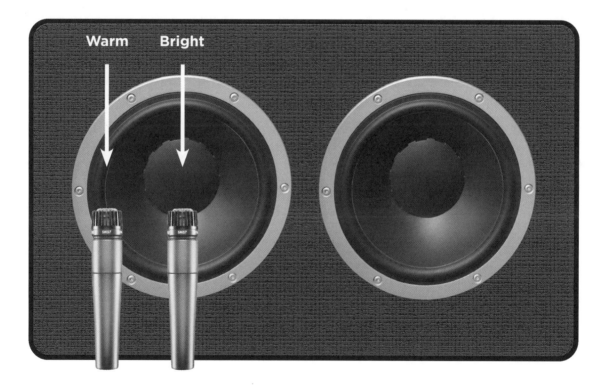

TIP: If the guitar rig has more than one speaker, have the guitarist play quietly so you can get close and listen to the speakers. There is usually one that sounds better than the others. You might even discover that the voice coil is noisy on one of the speakers. Place the mic in front of the best-sounding speaker.

TECHNIQUE 29
Multiple Mics on Electric Guitar

OVERVIEW: A single mic placed skillfully on the guitar speaker cabinet is usually enough to get the job done. However, there are times when the song, producer, or guitarist is looking for something extra. Additional microphones can add interest and personality to the guitar sound. The success of this augmentation depends on how carefully the mics are positioned. It also depends on the sound quality of the room that the speaker cabinet is in.

CHALLENGE: As a rule, it's preferable to use as few mics as possible on a sound source. Every time a mic is added to the setup, the chances of destructive phase combinations increases. It's always important to check the sound of the multi-mic setup in mono. If there are phase problems, then the sound will change from full and impressive to small, thin, and hollow.

SOLUTION: Careful positioning of the mics is important. It's also important to listen in mono as you build the miking approach. It's okay to switch back and forth between mono and stereo for reference, but once the setup is close, find the positions that sound good in mono. It will always sound nice when you open it back up to stereo.

1. The importance of phase: When two mic capsules are as close together as possible—like they are in a coincident stereo miking technique—the sound source arrives at both mics at exactly the same point in the waveform. Therefore, they'll be completely in phase and working together to provide a sound that's focused and powerful, even in mono. But, if two mics are pointed at the same source and the capsules are separated from each other, then the source waveform resonates each capsule at a different point in the wave cycle. As long as the combination is heard in stereo, the sound will be acceptable. However, when the mix is summed to mono or the mics on that instrument are summed to mono for location in the stereo mix pan, some frequency component will be out of phase. The resulting sound is likely to be hollow and weak.

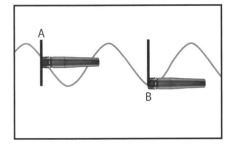 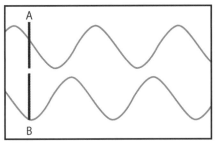 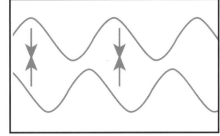

At the speed of sound, mics A and B capture the same waveform at two different points in the cycle. *At the speed of electron flow, the mixer receives the signal from each mic at exactly the same time.* *In mono, the opposing energies fight each other resulting in a different sound and wave shape.*

2. Stereo amplifier and cabinet: Some guitar amplifiers are stereo, and the speaker cabinet contains two speakers—one for each channel. In this scenario, it's very effective to simply use a microphone to capture the sound from each speaker. Pan the two mics hard left and right in the mix for an impressive stereo guitar sound.

3. Distant mic: A distant mic located between 2 and 6 feet from the speaker cabinet can add character and personality to the electric guitar sound. Either a high-quality tube condenser mic or a ribbon mic will typically work well in this application. Depending on the room sound and the way the close and distant mics sum together, it might work fine to just blend the two sounds together. If the mono summed tracks sound weak and hollow, either move the distant mic until the sound focuses and becomes solid or slide the distant mic track forward in the DAW until it's in phase with the close mic. This technique works particularly well 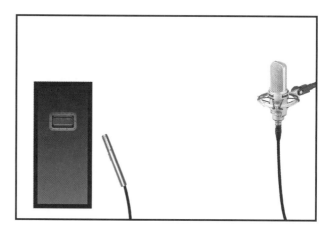 when the guitar is tracked as an overdub. But, when the band is recorded live, shifting the timing of the distant guitar mic can negatively affect the phase of other instruments in the same space.

4. Mono and stereo room mics: Room mics typically positioned between 10 and 20 feet from the source add room sound to the close mics in a similar way that reverb adds depth, complexity, and interest. Negative effects from problematic phase relationships aren't so much of an issue because of the amount of distance between the close mic and the room mic(s).

5. Two different mics on the same speaker: It can be effective to place two different mics on the same speaker at the same distance. Position the mics to capture different sounds from the speaker, record the two mics to different tracks, and then create the blend of the two mics that works best for the music during mixdown. Try using a dynamic mic aimed at the dust cover along with a ribbon mic closer to the outer edge of the cone. That'll provide a very aggressive high end from the dynamic mic and a very warm tone from the ribbon mic. Alternatively, swap the mic positions to capture a warmer high end from the ribbon aimed at the dust cover and a slightly aggressive warm tone from the dynamic mic on the cone.

6. Multiple rooms: Create an apparently larger space by opening doors and placing mics in the rooms surrounding the space where the guitar amp is located. As the sound makes its way around corners and down hallways, the apparent size of the recording space will increase dramatically. We used this technique on drums too. It can work well on any source with substantial volume—enough to fill up the surrounding rooms as well as the source room.

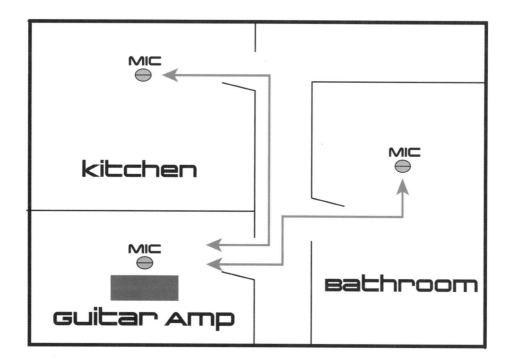

TIP: To get an aggressive sound from the amp at a lower volume, try this Eddie Van Halen trick: Plug the AC from the amp into a Variac power supply. This commercial power control can turn down the AC power feed to the amp. Turn the amp up as the power turns down to 50 or 60 percent.

TECHNIQUE 30
Electric Guitar Effects

OVERVIEW: Fact 1—Guitarists like to tinker with their gadgets. Fact 2—The guitarist's sound provides the inspiration required to get excited about the music he or she is making. Fact 3—An uninspired guitarist tends to create an uninspired guitar track.

CHALLENGE: Whether building a pedal board with stomp boxes or routing plug-ins inside a multi-effects processor or computer, there are certain guidelines that are helpful to follow or to intentionally ignore (for creative reasons, of course). It is rarely fruitful to randomly order the effects when creating a guitar sound. For example, it's standard to reverberate the distorted guitar sound. But, distorting the reverberated sound results in a radically different sound and musical statement. Our challenge in capturing electric guitar sounds lies in knowing how they are built. Once we understand the typical approach, then we can make better-informed decisions about where a deviation might be worth the risk.

SOLUTION: It's very helpful to know something about the tools that guitarists use to build their sounds. Here are some of the most common guitar effects and how they can be used to build a guitar sound:

1. **Noise Gate:** Guitars are typically prone to picking up noises, buzzes, and clacks—especially guitars with single-coil pickups. The noise gate is essentially a level control that turns the signal off when it's below a user-adjusted threshold. The goal is to set the threshold so that all intended notes and sounds happen as if there were no gate, but between those sounds and notes the guitar is silent. Gates are usually placed at the beginning of the effects chain before compressors. Distortion effects decrease the dynamic range so much that it is next to impossible to set the threshold.

2. **Compressor:** Compressors squeeze (compress, squash, cram, compact, stuff, etc.) the guitar's dynamic range, decreasing the distance between the quiet and loud sounds. Most guitar compressors are pretty simple. They essentially put a lid on the loudest sounds and let the user push the signal up against that lid (threshold). The result is that the signal doesn't exceed a set level but all of the quiet sounds are louder. Most guitarists love this effect because it makes all of their hammer-ons and pull-offs sound strong, clean, and much more impressive than they would be without the compressor.

3. **Distortion:** Distortion is what happens when a signal is overdriven. Distortion is a little like compression in that, at a certain point, the signal won't get much louder; it will just distort more. The drive control pushes (drives) the signal harder into the input, causing more distortion. However, this all happens at the input stage, so the resulting distorted sound can be turned up or down by the output control without changing the amount or intensity of the distortion. In effect, distortion lets the guitarist sound like the amp has been turned up to "11" even though the actual volume is quiet.

4. **Delay:** Delay simply copies the sound at the input and plays it back later. It simulates the size of the perceived room where the guitarist is performing because the human brain gets its cue for the size of the acoustic space from the initial reflection. So the length of the delay tells the brain at least a little bit about the environment. Since sound travels at about 1126 ft./sec. (not accounting for temperature, altitude, and such), it travels 1.126 ft./ms. So, if the guitarist selects a 300 ms delay, then we can easily calculate the distance sound travels at 300 ms as 300 divided by 1.126, which equals 266.43 feet. The brain deduces that the sound has traveled about 266 feet—the length to the end of the room and back—so it perceives a room that's roughly 133 feet long. The **feedback** control loops the delay back to the input, so the more feedback, the greater the number of delays. Typically, each delay gets a little quieter with a little less high-frequency content.

5. **Amp Simulator:** There's just something about a real guitar plugged into a real classic guitar amp that's magical. Sure, you can plug the output of your stompboxes or multi-effects processor straight into a recording interface or live mixer, but there will be something missing in the tone without including a guitar amp or a digital model of a guitar amp. Thankfully, there are several stompboxes that emulate great amps, speakers, and multi-effects devices like those from Line 6, Fractal, Boss, and others. Many of these devices let the user select the perfect amp with the perfect speakers, and they even offer options for mic choice and placement.

6. **VCO Delay Effects:** Three common guitar effects devices are the **chorus**, **flanger**, and **phase shifter**. Many guitarists use these effects, but few really understand their similarities and differences. All three effects rely on a voltage controlled oscillator (**VCO**). The VCO varies a delay of the original signal above and below the delay frequency; that oscillated delay is combined with the source signal. The result is a sweeping series of modulated harmonics that sweep up and down with the sped-up and slowed-down delay. The difference between these effects is simply in the length of the delay being oscillated. Chorus effects modulate a delay of about 25–35 ms. Flanger effects modulate a delay between about 3–15 ms. Phase shifter effects modulate a delay of about 1 ms or less. The speed and depth controls on each of these effects control the speed and depth of the VCO.

7. **Reverb:** Since the fundamental goal of reverberation has been to simulate an acoustical environment, it has historically been the last effect in the chain. Most classic guitar amps include an on-board spring reverb—yes, it's an actual spring in a metal box that is stimulated by the guitar sound, picked up, and blended with the dry guitar sound. Even though reverb is usually about playing the final guitar sound in a larger-sounding space, that doesn't mean it's not worth experimenting with.

TIP: There are historical and technical reasons that guitar effects tend to follow a consistent connection scheme. For the guitarist using stompboxes, there isn't much song-to-song flexibility. However, when using a multi-effects processor, experiment to break the mold and find your own sound. Reverberating distortion has a radically different creative impact than distorting reverberation. Mix it up!

TECHNIQUE 31
Electric Guitar Through a DI

OVERVIEW: The ways that guitar sounds are captured have, on one hand, remained constant since the early recordings, but on the other hand, have changed radically. DAW plug-ins, guitar multi-effects processors, and digital modeling have opened an entirely new array of creative possibilities.

CHALLENGE: An electric guitar plugged straight into an interface or other recorder input doesn't sound good. There are few absolutes in recording, but that's one of them. However, tracking the guitar straight into a DI that's connected to a recorder input frequently saves the day when it's time for mixdown. It's important that, whenever possible, the tracking engineer captures options that will be helpful in the mixdown process.

SOLUTION: Here are a few techniques and procedures that capture a great sound but still leave flexibility during mixdown:

1. It's all about the guitarist: When tracking a band, the engineer needs to rely on the guitarist's performance and sound-shaping skills. Many bands have excellent (or at least adequate) guitarists, largely because pop, rock, blues, and country music is frequently built around the guitarists and their sounds. But, if there's a struggle getting the best performance and the sounds don't seem to be right, consider hiring a studio guitarist. Hire the very best player—a player entrenched in the genre you're tracking and someone who has a reputation for creating inspired, great-sounding guitar tracks. He or she will be well worth their fee. Great players bring great instincts, excellent musical taste, experience creating custom sounds that support a musical vision, and great gear (in peak performance condition) to every session.

2. Connect the pedal board to the DI: In many performance situations, the guitarist's only practical option is to connect to the mixer through a DI straight out of the pedal board. Because of this, they might have tweaked their direct sounds to perfection. Listen to the sounds. Sometimes, when time is tight, it's acceptable to record direct from the pedal board output even though there might be a better way, given more time.

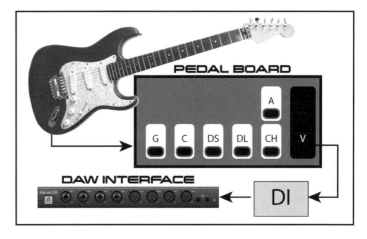

3. Stereo Outputs: Most multi-effects processors provide stereo outputs. When tracking in stereo from a multi-effects processor, simply connect the left and right outputs to the inputs of a stereo DI and then connect the DI outputs to two channels of the recording device.

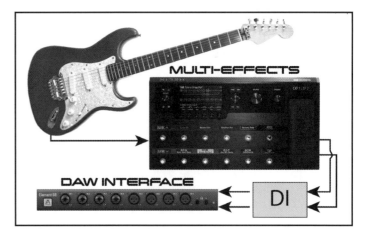

4. Mono Outputs: Sometimes, it's necessary to use a mono output from a stereo multi-effects processor—as when connecting to a mono guitar amp. Usually, the jack that's meant to send a mono signal is marked on the output. Sometimes both of the jacks are marked for mono. Use the mono output, or you might end up with a signal that's been delayed 20 ms and is 90 percent reverb!

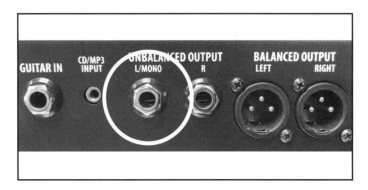

5. Connect the guitar to the DI: It's always a good idea to record the direct signal straight from the guitar, because guitar effects plug-ins work just as well on the signal that comes straight out of the recorder as they do coming straight out of the guitar. Even if you're not sure how or if you'll use the direct signal, it's a lifesaver when you need it.

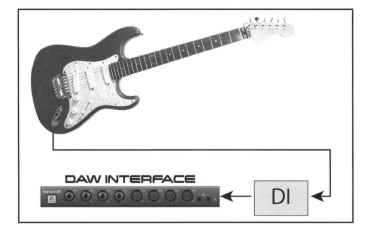

6. Optimal flexibility: If time and resources permit, try the all-of-the-above approach. Record the DI straight from the guitar, connect the thru output from the first DI to the pedal board input, and then connect the output from the pedal board to the DAW interface.

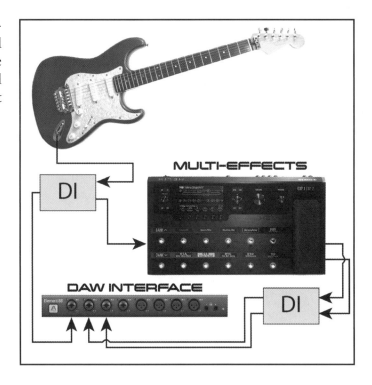

TIP: When the guitarist is a true virtuoso and he or she has built the guitar sounds specifically to fit the music, then there's nothing wrong with committing the sounds to the recorder. It's not always a good thing to save hundreds of options for the mix because it can cause what Quincy Jones calls "the paralysis from analysis!"

TECHNIQUE 32
Stereo Electric Guitar

OVERVIEW: There are a lot of ways to capture great mono guitar sounds. There are arguably even more ways to capture stereo guitar sounds.

CHALLENGE: It always comes down to a musical decision—how big does the electric guitar really need to be in the mix? Imagine the sound of an excellent vocalist delivering an excellent performance of a great song, dry in the mix and positioned right in your face—maybe right inside your head! Then support that with a fantastic acoustic guitar performance, clean and dry. Now, that's powerful, but only when it's right for the song. Often, we reach first for delay and reverb to make something sound impressive. However, we need to listen first to the tempo, notes, lyrics, and heart of the song to help us choose which way to go.

SOLUTION: Here are some techniques for tracking stereo electric guitar sounds:

1. Pedal board outputs: With a simple stompbox pedal board, the guitar signal typically stays mono from the output of the guitar to the output of the pedal board. Then, the output from the pedal board is connected to the singe input of an amplifier. That's really how it's been done for decades, but there are definitely a lot of very large and impressive guitar sounds recorded throughout the '60s, '70s, '80s, '90s, and beyond.

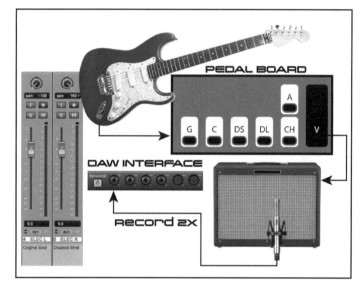

2. Double tracking to the rescue: First, create a great-sounding mono guitar tone. Next, play the same part twice to two separate tracks. Pan the tracks apart for a very large and impressive sound. As the two tracks play against each other, it's the imperfections that make the sound interesting and powerful.

3. Electronic doubling: Use a digital delay to electronically double-track a single mono guitar track. Route the recorded guitar track to the input of a delay and set the delay time to between about 11 and 35 ms. Make sure the delay is set for a single repeat, and then pan the original to one side and the delay to the other side. Base the exact delay time on two factors: 1) Does it sound good in the mix? 2) Does it still sound full when monitored in mono?

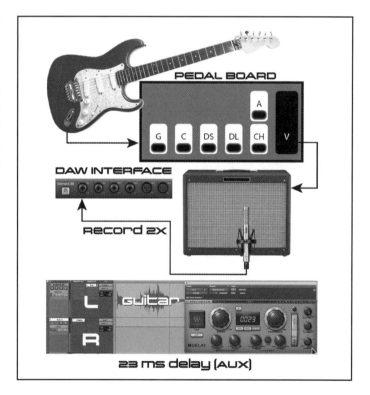

4. Stereo multi-effects processor to stereo amps: Virtually all multi-effects processors provide stereo outputs. The stereo sounds in a multi-effects device are usually a result of stereo reverberation devices, stereo delays, stereo choruses, and so on. But they're also frequently a result of assigning one modeled amp to the left and a different modeled amp to the right—often with one of the amps delayed slightly. These setups are usually very wide- and impressive-sounding. To take this setup to the next level, connect the left and right outputs to two separate amplifiers and mic their speaker cabinets.

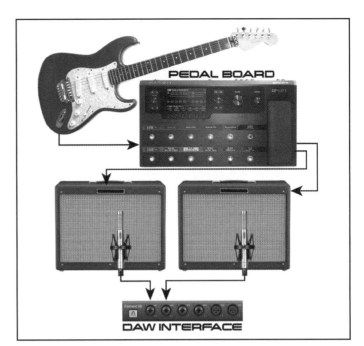

5. The Kitchen Sink: When time and resources permit, combine the techniques we've covered thus far. You're likely to find a huge and impressive sound, but be forewarned that you might reach a point of diminishing returns. Avoid adding more and more sounds just for the sake of more, more, and more. Build guitar tones that sound great in the specific musical context.

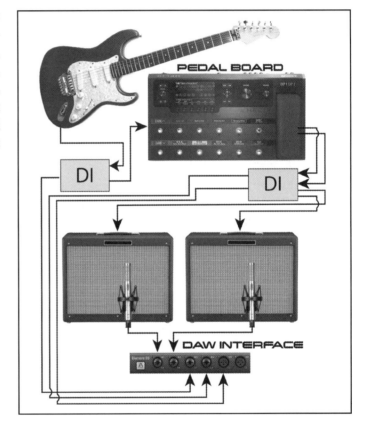

TIP: Once you've decided on all of the basic sound components and initial panning, monitor the sound in mono. It doesn't matter how huge and impressive the stereo guitar tone is when your song is played over a mono sound system and the guitar is missing or just sounds awful. If you create an appealing sound in mono, than it certainly will sound great in stereo.

TECHNIQUE 33
Grand Piano

OVERVIEW: Grand piano is a wonderful instrument. It contains virtually all of the commonly used musical range of pitches and has a rich, full tone that's tough to beat.

CHALLENGE: Before tracking, make sure that the piano is perfectly in tune. Hire a professional piano tuner before the session. Piano is far too difficult to tune on your own—it's not a DIY task. It's also important that the piano is in good working condition and that the strings aren't dull and lifeless. Piano is most difficult to record in the same room with other instruments because it can be pretty loud. Because the mics are usually placed inside an open lid, they can catch virtually every other instrument in the room.

SOLUTION: Here are a few techniques and procedures that capture a great piano sound:

1. Mic choice: The piano sound contains a lot of transient content because the hammers strike the strings, so small- and large-diaphragm condenser microphones are the most popular choices for tracking piano. Small-diaphragm mics typically have a full-bandwidth frequency response and an extremely accurate transient response. Large diaphragm mics still capture very clean transients but tend to roll off in the highs above 15 or 16 kHz so they sometimes feel slightly warmer. Common condenser microphone choices for tracking piano are the AKG 451, Neumann U 87, Neumann M 149, Audio-Technica AT4041, and AKG 414. Ribbon microphones are also a great choice when the piano sound needs to be warmer and fuller. Common ribbon microphone choices for tracking piano are the Royer R-122, Royer SF-12, Royer SF-24, Coles 4038, and Audio-Technica AT4080.

2. Recording levels: The piano sound contains more transient content than one might think. Piano hammers are voiced for a brighter or darker sound. Usually, the piano technician uses a voicing needle that softens the hammers by roughing and fluffing the hammers. Sometimes, when a piano sound is too dark or dull, the piano technician applies a lacquer to the hammers, making them harder and therefore increasing the brightness of the piano sound. Even when the hammers are voiced for a warmer sound, leave plenty of headroom. Record at 24-bit 48-kHz audio to increase the vertical audio resolution so there's no urgency about tracking the piano sound as hot as possible.

3. It's all about the song: Some songs require a strong low end—others don't. As a tracking engineer, assess what the music needs. If the piano part is big and bombastic with a strong left hand, then it makes sense to make sure that the high and low ranges are separate and powerful. If the piano part focuses primarily on the mid and high ranges, then it makes more sense to adjust the mic placement to best capture those ranges.

4. One high and inside and one low and away: With the lid propped open with the long stick, place one mic 12–18 inches above the high strings over the hammers. Place the second mic over the low strings at the far end of the piano. This technique gets a wide and impressive sound. But, when the mics are panned hard left and right, the left-hand (low) side tends to read much hotter on the meter for the same trim setting.

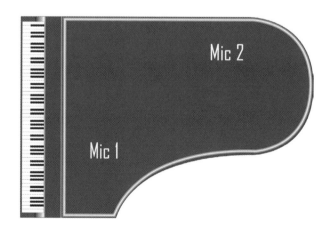

5. High and low over the hammers: This technique is more natural-sounding than the previous technique, but the exact positions should be adjusted to fit the range and energy of the song. Place both mics over the hammers from a distance of 12–18 inches.

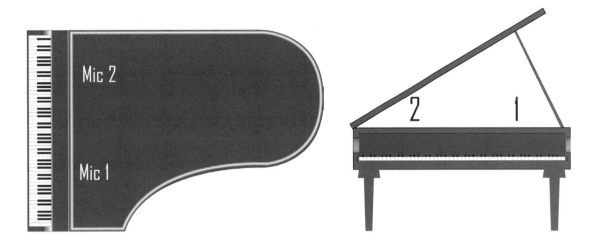

6. X-Y at the lid opening: Place a stereo X-Y pair of condenser mics at the opening with the lid on the high stick or low stick.

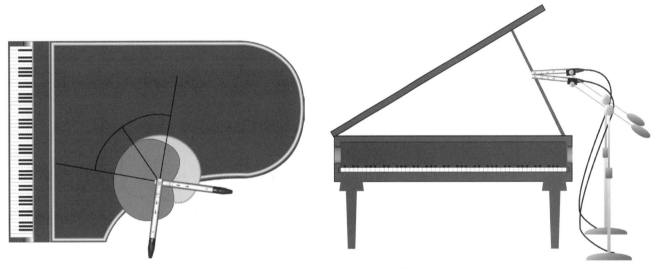

7. Creating isolation: Use a thick blanket to cover the piano lid opening. This helps keep unwanted leakage out of the piano mics, and it tones down the leakage from the piano into other mics in the same room.

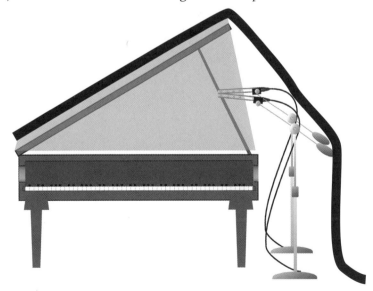

TIP: Imagine the piano sound that you'll need in mixdown. That'll help you focus on what's necessary. If the song doesn't demand a large, full-range piano sound, then it's better to focus on getting just the right sound for the music than to spend time trying to capture a great solo sound.

OVERVIEW: The Fender Rhodes electric piano was released in 1965, but it really became most popular in the 1970s. It had a warm sound that was easy to blend with the rest of the instruments in the band. It covered the parts a grand piano would cover, and it was very portable, especially compared to a grand piano! The Wurlitzer electric piano (sometimes referred to as a "Wurly") was released in the same era as the Rhodes. Though the sounds of the Rhodes and Wurlitzer are similar enough to fill the same function, they are different enough to be easily distinguishable.

CHALLENGE: The classic Rhodes piano sat on top of its speaker cabinet, and the four speakers in the cabinet (two facing front and two facing back) were wired to pan back and forth to create a tremolo effect—that's the classic Rhodes sound. The sounds of the Rhodes, Wurlitzer, and B-3 are easily sampled or recreated in a synthesizer, but the sound of a player laying into the real instruments is hard to beat. Most people won't be tracking these classic instruments, but almost everyone will track their sounds via any modern keyboard.

SOLUTION: Here are a few techniques and procedures that help capture great electric piano and organ sounds:

1. The Rhodes Suitcase Model: The Rhodes Suitcase electric piano started the electric piano craze. The keyboard and electronics were designed to sit on the speaker cabinet. The rich Rhodes tone came from the four speakers and two stereo amps built into the cabinet. Two speakers pointed forward toward the audience, and two identical speakers faced backward at the player. The characteristic Rhodes sound used the tremolo feature where the sound panned back and forth from left to right and back. Use a dynamic mic such as the Shure SM57 or Beta 57 on each of the front (audience side) speakers and record them to separate tracks to retain the ability to pan the tremolo sounds during mixdown. Miking the back speakers works, but there is an increased chance of picking up too much pedal noise. Be sure to locate the speakers when placing the mics. They staggered from upper to lower for a good fit and an even sound on both sides off the cabinet. On the player's side, the right speaker is higher and the left speaker is lower. Use a small flashlight to look through the grille to locate the speakers. As with all speakers, the brightest sound is at the center of the dust cover, and the warmest sound is at the outer edge of the cone. Aim the mics accordingly for the desired tone.

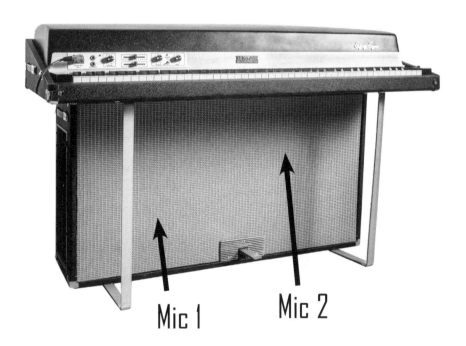

Mic 1   Mic 2

2. The Rhodes Stage Model: The Suitcase Rhodes lacked tonal flexibility, and the speaker cabinet was a little cumbersome to cart around. So Fender eventually released the Rhodes Stage model. It was essentially the same keyboard mechanism without the speaker cabinet. It could be connected to a normal amplifier or direct into the mixer, giving the player more control over the sound and one less speaker cabinet to carry. Unlike the Suitcase model, the Stage Rhodes has a mono output. But, when connected to a stereo mixer in the studio or on stage, the back and forth panning effect is simple to recreate with any multi-effects processor. The effect is usually called **auto-pan**. To track the Stage Rhodes, simply connect the output to a DI. To increase the tonal interest, use the DI's thru jack to connect to an amplifier and mic the cabinet.

3. The Wurlitzer: The Wurlitzer electric piano came out at about half the price of the Fender Rhodes. It was much more lightweight than the Rhodes and had an obviously similar tone, but just different enough to be unique. Originally an alternative to the Rhodes, the Wurlitzer sound eventually came to be preferred by many musicans in certain genres over the cleaner and slightly more polished sound of the Rhodes. As with most vintage gear, there's an ebb and flow to popularity, but there's never a doubt what is meant when someone asks for a Wurlitzer sound or a Rhodes sound. The Wurly has a mono output. Use a DI to connect it to a mixer and use the thru jack on the DI to connect it to an amp for more interest. One thing the Wurlitzer has that the Rhodes doesn't is an on-board speaker, making it perfect for teaching lessons, practicing at home, or writing music.

> **TIP:** Electric pianos sound great through many effects, such as reverberation, stereo chorus, flanger, delays, and even distortion. Experiment! Discover all the possibilities that these wonderful classic instruments offer.

TECHNIQUE 35
Organ

OVERVIEW: There are a few classic organ sounds that define genres, grooves, and emotions. The Hammond B-3 through a Leslie speaker cabinet is by far the most important modern-day organ sound. The Hammond Organ Company, in business since 1935, created many portable electronic organs, but with the introduction of the B-3 and its added harmonic percussion circuit in 1954, it's the model that became the go-to keyboard for blues, R&B, reggae, and rock. However, it shouldn't be overlooked that, around the world, there are countless churches and concert halls with monstrously large pipe organs built right into the buildings. Although it's infrequent that anyone other than an engineer who specializes in recording these amazing instruments will get the call, it might happen, so we'll take a quick look at a few considerations that will be helpful if you get the opportunity.

CHALLENGE: The Hammond B-3 sound is amazingly full and powerful. But, a B-3 virtually always uses a Leslie speaker cabinet to deliver its sound. The Leslie has moving speakers, so there's a bit of a challenge in capturing the full sound along with the Leslie effect. When recording a pipe organ, there are several considerations about miking an instrument that might be 50+ feet wide and 70+ feet tall—some pipe organs even have various registers located strategically around the facility.

SOLUTION: Here are a few consideration for miking the B-3 and pipe organs:

1. Basic functionality of the Hammond B-3: The B-3 uses a series of drawbars along the top of the upper keyboard to shape the tone. Each drawbar controls the level of a single harmonic. The pure tones controlled by each drawbar work together to create interesting and compelling sounds. The harmonic percussion circuit introduced by Hammond with the B-3 model adds an interesting percussive element to the beginning of each note, creating a sound that—in the hands of a great player—locks into any great groove and is very supportive in the overall rhythm section. The B-3 contains a full pedal board, so the organist can play the bass parts with his or her feet while comping out chords and playing solo licks. There are 12 color-inverted keys to the left of each keyboard—the keys that are normally white are black and the keys that are normally black are white. These keys don't make sound. Instead, they are presets for different ranges of drawbars.

The legendary Hammond B-3 was a game changer.

2. The Leslie Speaker Cabinet: The Leslie speaker cabinet contains two sets of rotating speakers. The organ output is split into highs and lows. The highs are sent to the two-speed rotating horns in the upper half of the cabinet, and the lows are sent to the two-speed rotating woofer baffle in the lower portion of the cabinet. It's the sound of these ranges spinning around, speeding up, and slowing down that gives the B-3 a magical sound—a sound that brings life and motion to virtually every song that's played through them. It's not the actual speakers that move. The high-end speaker aims upward and is funneled into a tube that feeds into two metal cones. The sound from the speaker comes out of the cones, which are often referred to as "horns." The woofer faces downward into a large round baffle that's closed off most of the way around except for a port that projects the sound. The Leslie is frequently miked with a single cardioid

dynamic mic on the horns and another single cardioid dynamic mic on the woofer. This is efficient, and in a live setting, getting close to the components helps with isolation. There are slat openings around the top and bottom of the cabinet to project the sound from the horns all the way around the cabinet. It's also a good idea to put two mics on the horns directly across the cabinet from each other. In the studio, try moving the mics a little farther from the cabinet. Omnidirectional mics can also be a good choice in a great-sounding room. Send all of the mics to separate recorder channels so that the sound can be fine-tuned for the music.

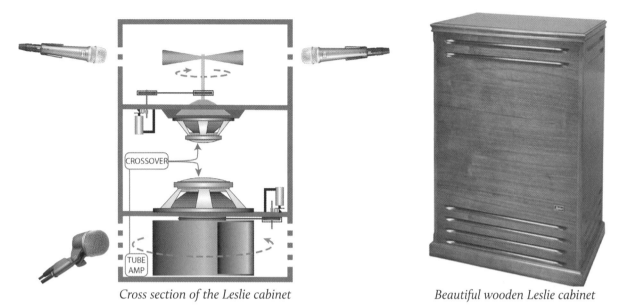

Cross section of the Leslie cabinet *Beautiful wooden Leslie cabinet*

3. Pipe Organ: The traditional pipe organ is an amazing instrument. It's typically an integral part of the construction of the hall with a massive sound originating from a massively sized area. Close miking is out of the question, but there are a few approaches that make sense and produce great results. You can never go wrong in any recording situation by walking around the venue and the instrument to find the spot that sounds best to your own ears. You should be able to place a stereo pair of mics or a surround setup at that location and get a great recording. However, most recordings in this setting are from live performances. That can be problematic because the location you choose is probably right in the sweet spot for the noisy, sneezing, coughing, candy-wrapper-crackling audience. An excellent approach to miking the pipe organ is to place a stereo pair of high-quality condenser microphones on a high stand that can be positioned right in front of the pipes and far enough out to get a good stereo balance. A spaced pair of omnidirectional mics about 1 meter apart will capture a great sound. Also, a small-diaphragm condenser mic is a good choice in an ORTF configuration. Mics such as the Schoeps MK-2, Neumann M 50 or M 149, or the Neumann KM 84 or KM 184 are first-choice mics in this setting. But, any good omni or cardioid condenser mic is capable of capturing a great sound.

Our Lady of the Visitation Church, Montech Tarn-et-Garonne gallery organ

TIP: The Hammond B-3 sounds great distorted through a tube amp or through a high-quality distortion plug-in. In its raw form and at loud volumes, the B-3 tube amp has a nice, warm distortion sound. On the back of the cabinet, the horns and woofer rotor are exposed, which makes it easier to position the mics.

TECHNIQUE 36
Synthesizers

OVERVIEW: The word "synthesizer" encompasses a vast range of sounds—virtually all of them! If you include subtractive, additive, and sample-based synthesizers, then any instrument or sound can be produced, tweaked, and endlessly morphed into new creations that no ear has heard before.

CHALLENGE: To offer tips for tracking synthesizers is a bit like offering tips to track all sounds; however, there are some techniques that we can apply to support the sounds being produced. We need to decide whether to run the synth through a DI, into an amp, or a combination of several approaches together.

SOLUTION: Here are a few tips that can help track high-quality, musically supportive synth sounds:

1. Amp or no amp: Most of the time, a synthesizer sounds best running directly into the mixer. But, there are times when an amp is convenient or necessary. For a rehearsal with other instruments and no mixer, an amp is necessary. Sometimes, the sound of the room adds to the sound of the synth—another situation where an amp is handy to have. Choose the keyboard amp wisely. The synth produces an extremely wide range of frequencies that is typically beyond what an amp designed for guitar can handle. Use an amp that's specially designed for use with a keyboard if you want to hear the full range of the synth sound. If you don't have access to a keyboard amplifier, it's OK to use a bass amp because it can handle the low-frequency content, but the highs will probably lack presence.

2. Stereo or mono: Most synths have a stereo output with one of the channels marked for mono use. The mono channels sum the layered sounds and effects to mono rather than just outputting the left or right alone. This is convenient since a lot of patches are built with various sounds and effects panned across the left-right panorama. Taking the discrete left or right channel might provide a sound that's nothing like the intended sound. It's almost always best to track the stereo output from the synth through a DI or into an instrument-level input. There is definitely a case for tracking mono instruments such as bass guitar and individual instruments in mono. However, those instruments are often generated in mono from the stereo outputs—identical signals on the left and right. Of course, if tracks are getting scarce, track in mono wherever it's possible.

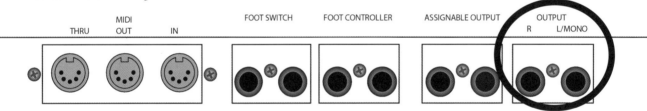

Most keyboards have stereo outputs with one channel designated for mono use.

3. Using an active, passive, or a tube DI: A synthesizer provides a full-range output that can be as hyped in the high end or beefy in the low end as the sound designer wants. To get the most faithful transfer of the sound from the synth outputs, use a high-quality passive DI such as the stereo version of the Radial JDI. If you want to add some low- and high-end punch to the synth sound, then use a high-quality active DI such as the stereo version of the Radial J48 or the Countryman Type 85. For a warm, aggressive sound, try a high-quality tube DI like the Radial Firefly or the Demeter VTDB-2b Tube Direct.

4. Miking the amplifier: When using a keyboard amplifier, there are often multiple speakers in the cabinet that cover different frequency ranges. Close-miking, like one might do with a single-speaker guitar or bass cabinet, doesn't work well with a multiple-speaker keyboard. To capture the full range of frequencies, move the mic a few feet away from the cabinet. The exact placement will depend on the size of the cabinet, volume level, other instruments that might leak into the synth mic, and how much room sound you want on the recording. Since the keyboard amp is more of a high-fidelity playback device, try using a condenser mic to capture a more accurate recording.

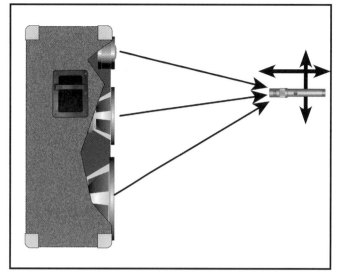

Move the mic back and forth and up and down to locate the position that captures the best balance.

5. Reamping and recording the room: A technique that's commonly used for guitar sounds is **reamping**. Technically, the term reamping refers to the process of recording dry guitar parts without effects to the recording device and then playing them back with plug-in effects through an amplifier and miking those sounds to new recorded tracks. With a synthesizer, the sounds are typically fine-tuned once they're recorded, but there is a lot that can be gained by sending them to an amplification system in the studio and miking the sound that the room adds. Whereas reamping involves miking the amp (and possibly the room) that plays the new sounds created from the dry guitar track, synthesizer sounds are all about miking the room sound. It's not necessary to mic the amplification system, whether that be a keyboard amp or high-quality stereo studio monitors. In fact, cardioid mics can be aimed away from the speakers, or depending on the room, omnidirectional mics are a great choice. This technique adds a lot of realism and energy to the synth sounds, and there's nothing that says you can't add plug-ins to create a new sound to reamp at the same time.

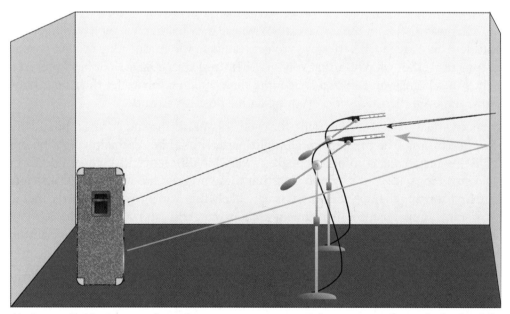

Aiming cardioid mics away from the amp captures more of the room sound. Aim the backs of the cardioid pattern at the amp for the most off-axis rejection. The mics are focused on the reflections, so moving them farther from the wall but closer to the amp can make the room sound larger.

TIP: Get the most out of your keyboard tracking by connecting it to the mixer through a stereo DI, while at the same time connecting the thru jack on the DI to an amp in the studio and miking the studio room.

TECHNIQUE 37
Vocal Performance

OVERVIEW: It's all about the vocals, and it's all about the song. The singer and the song are so tightly intertwined that there's no separating them. If the vocals don't sound good—or at least deliver the emotional impact of the song—then the song won't be good. If the lyrics and melody aren't powerful, then it will be difficult to build a powerful and impacting production.

CHALLENGE: Singing is probably the most personal instrument of all. To vocalists, if you don't like their singing, it's akin to not liking them personally. The biggest challenge when working with vocalists is keeping them encouraged, confident, and in the game. They don't usually respond well to criticism, so it's necessary to find ways to communicate that help deliver their best performance.

SOLUTION: Here are a few pointers that I've learned that help singers deliver their best performances in a recording environment:

1. It's all about the mood: If the singer feels the environment, they're likely to feel the song. It's up to you to see that the environment they're in supports the emotions they need to feel in order to deliver a world-class performance. Adjust the lighting so it creates a mood that supports the performance. Get used to setting up Christmas lights and trees in the studio in June. Don't be afraid to bring in special lighting if the performance needs them. Michael Jackson worked best with the studio completely dark except for a a single pin-spot aimed straight down at the mic. When he wasn't singing, he wanted to dance around the studio without any inhibitions so that when it was time to sing, he was already 100-percent in the groove and ready to go. Make sure the temperature is perfect for the vocalist. As a tracking engineer, always be proactive. Ask the singer how they'd like the lighting and if the studio is too hot or cold. Great singers will probably ask for what they require to do their best work; however, inexperienced singers might not even realize what they need to deliver a great performance.

2. Keep a positive attitude at all times: Build the singer up and find ways to stoke the singer's confidence. Build trust with singers. They must know that you have their best interest in mind at all times, and they must believe that you are on their side. Find ways to support, encourage, and inspire the singer. This actually goes for all musicians, but the voice is a more personal instrument than most, so these points are extra critical when tracking vocals. Leave terms like "You're flat," "You're sharp," "Can't you feel the beat?," and "That was awful," home in the cat box where they belong. You will never get results with that kind of attitude. There are much better ways to get results in the studio. Once you've worked with a great singer for a long time, they will know that you love them and always have their best interest in mind. Once you've reached that point, you can be a little more direct in an effort to let the singer know what you're hearing. However, even then, deliver everything with a positive attitude.

3. The singer should be well rested: Make sure that you encourage the singer to get plenty of sleep and rest before the vocal session. The pre-session all-night party should be rescheduled to the post-session all-night party. Being rested and comfortable makes a very big difference in a singer's performance. Singers use large and small muscles, and it's important that these muscles are warmed up sufficiently and safely. When you're first starting to track sessions, it is very likely that you'll wear many hats, including engineer, producer, assistant, runner, janitor, instrument tech, psychiatrist, and vocal coach. Google "Vocal Warm-up Exercises" or purchase a good vocal technique book. Learn a few basic vocal warm-ups to help the vocalist perform better behind the mic.

4. Encourage the vocalist to be prepared and to learn the lyrics: Vocalists should know the lyrics well, and they should understand what the lyrics say and mean. Singers sell the song's emotional message to the listener and should therefore have the lyrics internalized in their soul.

5. Proper Technique: The time to work on vocal technique should be well in advance of the tracking session. Trying to change the way a vocalist sings while he or she is already nervous, insecure, and probably getting fatigued is a losing proposition. If the singer needs a teacher or a vocal coach to prepare for the session, then start the lessons a few months before the planned session date.

6. Pointers: It's all about the way you say it. After you've tracked several vocalists, you'll discover a few little things that make a big difference in the performance. These are rarely things that have to do with changes in vocal technique. They're often small changes that seem insignificant but can in fact be very helpful. Here are just a few things I've discovered that can make a big difference while not destroying the vocalist's confidence: 1) When a lyric ends with an "a," "e," or "i" sound and the pitch is flat, simply recommend that

the singer put a little more "e" sound in the word. That usually brings the pitch up to where it needs to be. A vocal coach might not use that technique, but it works in a session. 2) If the vocal intensity is sagging, then ask the singer to move more air when they sing. Most singers understand that, and it doesn't require them to fundamentally change how they sing. 3) If the vocalist is having a problem sustaining a note or singing a long phrase, then ask them to support a little more from the diaphragm. This is the same as suggesting moving more air. Singers tend to understand this, and it's a simple change. 4) Learn how to take a break. Often, we bludgeon through the session because we're low on time, we're anxious to finish, or we just haven't learned how to identify the point of no return. Most singers just aren't used to singing for hours and hours, especially in a situation that demands all of their mental and emotional energy in addition to the physical exertion that singing demands. I've never found a special ratio of singing time to break time because it's different for every singer. Some singers thrive on endless takes and retakes and will literally maintain stamina for hours. Other singers start to fade after a half hour. Be sensitive to the kind of rest each singer needs.

7. Attacks and releases: A good singer can attack the beginnings of each note with accuracy and energy, but it takes a great singer to release the notes perfectly. In fact, a vocal performance is more about releases than the rest of the notes. A great singer builds energy through the note in a way that delivers the listener personally to the heart of the next lyric. It's really quite amazing! Listen to great singers and pay close attention to the way they release every note. It's a game changer.

8. Listen to the vocalist's headphone mix: I've discovered that setting up an excellent headphone mix is likely the most important single thing you can provide for any singer in any session. If you hear a singer floating out of tune or out of the groove, then simply ask him or her how their headphone mix is. Consistently, a singer with a bad headphone mix delivers a sub-par performance. However, if they have a mix with just what they need, then they'll usually deliver a great performance. Always listen to the singer's mix, preferably through the same kind of headphones they're using. When you hear what the singer hears, it becomes pretty obvious how you as the tracking engineer can help capture a better vocal performance. If you hear the pitch getting a little off and you're hearing what they hear, then simply turn up a track with a solid pitch reference, and you will very likely hear them find the pitch perfectly. Often, the vocalist has turned up the synth pad for pitch reference, but that synth pad might have a low frequency oscillation (**LFO**) that's constantly sweeping the pitch above and below the actual pitch. Nobody can reference accurate pitch from that type of sound. However, if you turn that instrument down and turn up a natural grand piano, Rhodes, Wurlitzer, or acoustic guitar, then the singer will have a solid pitch reference and will lock onto the pitches immediately. If you're hearing the singer's headphone mix, then you can help them find the correct pitch without needing to stop the session. The same concept supports helping the singer find the rhythm. If the vocals aren't following the groove, then find something in the headphone mix that best defines the groove and turn that up, or alternatively, turn something down that's getting in the way of the groove.

9. The power of the take in the can: From the first note that squeaks out of the vocalist's cords, have the DAW in record! That first take is often the best. It's likely to have the most excitement, anticipation, emotion, and groove. Always be in record mode when tracking a singer, and at the end of the take, keep it and open a new layer on the vocal track. Have the vocalist sing the song straight through a few times without breaks. Record every take to a new layer or track. This helps the singer get warmed up at the very least, and these might be the best takes. When you're sure that you have a solid take all the way through the song, it's usually worth doing a take that focuses in on certain phrases. Some singers get better when this process starts; however, many singers just aren't comfortable with starting and stopping. They get frustrated, and at that point, you've lost them.

10. When fatigue sets in: For many vocalists, once fatigue sets in, the session is effectively over for the day. But, some singers just need a break during which they treat their voice carefully. The amazing vocal coach, Maestro David Kyle, prescribed lukewarm water and bananas to soothe the voice. The singer should avoid liquids that are too hot or too cold—no hot coffee or tea and no ice cold beverages.

11. Capturing a singer's best performance is more about relationship and trust than technique and perfection: It can take some time to build a relationship, but once the singer trusts themselves into your capable guidance, you can help them release the magic they feel inside for the song.

> **TIP:** This technique has no pictures. That's because singing is virtually all in the head of the singer. Confidence is extremely important. Singers must be mentally and emotionally prepared to deliver their best performance. If the song is angry and bombastic, help the singer feel that way. If the song is about puppy dogs and butterflies, find a way to inspire the singer to sing about puppies and butterflies!

TECHNIQUE 38
Vocal Mic Choice

OVERVIEW: The microphone is the singer's connection to the audience, whether in person or on recorded media—it's a very important consideration! The mic that's used to track a vocalist can make a big difference in the quality of the vocal performance, for some reasons you may or may not guess.

CHALLENGE: When tracking vocals, there are so many important variables. The quality of the mic is important, but we must always keep in mind that a great vocal performance is all about an inspired emotional delivery of a great song. Given the choice between tracking a mediocre performance from a vocalist on a world-class, vintage, classic, to-die-for mic and getting an inspired passionate performance through a mic that costs less than $100, choose the latter every time.

SOLUTION: Here are a few factors to consider when choosing a vocal microphone:

1. Live performances versus studio recordings: In a live performance application, there is quite a different set of considerations compared to a studio performance. Mics that are designed for live use, such as the Shure SM58 dynamic mic, take advantage of the proximity effect by rolling off the low-frequency band. They almost force the singer to move in close to the mic to get a full sound, helping to dramatically improve isolation. To achieve a full vocal sound, the singer typically needs to be within a couple inches of the mic capsule. Singers with great mic technique take advantage of the proximity effect by moving closer to the mic for the dramatic, sensitive lyrics while backing off for the louder, aggressive passages. On the other hand, mics designed for use in the studio have a low end that extends into the low frequency band, enabling the capture of a full-sounding vocal from 6 to 12 inches or more. When using a more distant technique, the sound of the actual room dramatically impacts the recorded sound. Therefore, most mics designed for recording vocals provide a high-pass filter, which lets the singer move in closer to the mic without capturing a vocal sound that is overly thick and boomy. In addition to providing better separation from other musicians in the same room, the high-pass filter lets the singer move in closer to the mic for a warm and intimate tone.

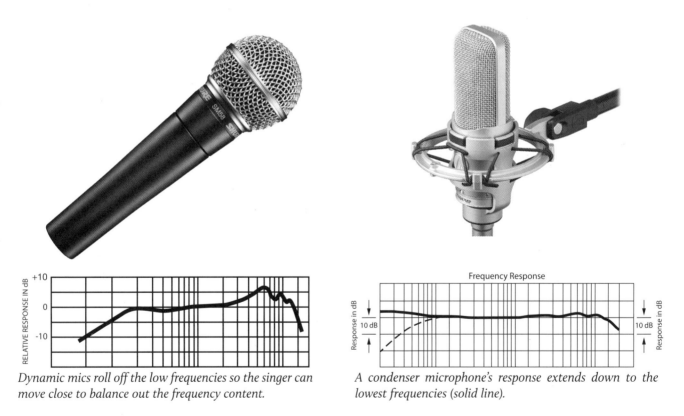

Dynamic mics roll off the low frequencies so the singer can move close to balance out the frequency content.

A condenser microphone's response extends down to the lowest frequencies (solid line).

2. Test multiple microphones: Every mic brings a different set of strengths to the vocal session. Just because a mic is a large-diaphragm condenser mic doesn't dictate that it will sound great on the vocalist that you're tracking on a given day. Set three or four likely choices in a row and try each of them on the vocalist. Record each mic to a separate DAW track so you can listen closely to the recorded sound. Some people like to set up multiple mics placed very close together in front of the singer, performing this test in one take. I've found that the assessment is more reliable when you set them up one at a time through the same channel and processing. This is especially true when using analog hardware.

3. Condenser microphones: Vocal sounds contain many facets ranging from the transients produced by sibilant sounds to the sound of the air moving over the vocal cords to the way the vocal cords vibrate. There's a lot of detail in the vocal performance that can be captured most faithfully by a condenser microphone. Either a small- or large-diaphragm microphone is capable of capturing the detail in a vocal sound. However, mics that are considered great vocal mics usually have a large diaphragm because they capture a vocal sound with a bit more warmth and depth relative to a small-diaphragm condenser mic.

4. Setting the high-pass filter: Many large-diaphragm condenser microphones provide a multi-position high-pass filter. The AKG 414 XLII has a three-position high-pass filter with settings for 40 Hz, 80 Hz, and 160 Hz. Some mics have multi-position filters, each with a different character and function. For example, the Shure KSM 44 has a two-position high-pass filter, but each filter has a different slope. Its 80 Hz cut-off filter has an 18 dB per octave slope, but its 115 Hz roll-off filter has a 6 dB per octave slope. Make sure you read the documentation that comes with each mic to understand the best uses for each function.

The AKG 414 XLII provides three high-pass filter settings. Use these when the singer wants to get close to the mic. As the singer gets closer, raise the HPF frequency.

The Shure KSM44 has two HPFs. The 80 Hz filter cuts off at 18 dB per octave. The 115 dB filter rolls off at 6 dB per octave.

5. Pop Filters/Windscreens: Condenser mics are very sensitive to blasts of air like the excessive air movement caused by the pronunciation of the plosives in the letters "p" and "b." These plosives cause a pop, which is the sound of the diaphragm bottoming out—a sound that's difficult to get rid of. Because of this, it is usually necessary to place an acoustically transparent wind block between the singer and the microphone. Some windscreens are made from a foam rubber material that fits over the top end of the side-address microphone. Another type of windscreen uses a nylon material over a hoop to block the wind made by plosives. Most engineers prefer the nylon hoop pop filters because they tend to be more acoustically transparent than the thick foam filter. Some singers who are experienced in the studio are able to record without the use of a windscreen—they simply aim the plosive off the mic diaphragm. In addition to diffusing the air aimed at the diaphragm, the windscreen also keeps the singer at a controlled distance from the mic.

Foam windscreen (above). Nylon hoop windscreen (right).

TIP: Find the technique that makes the singer comfortable. Some singers want to hold the mic because that's what they're used to. Frank Sinatra insisted on using a handheld wireless mic on one of his classic albums. Some singers can't sing while wearing headphones, which means there must be monitors in the studio while the vocals are tracked! Face them back at the singer and use a cardioid mic. No problem!

TECHNIQUE 39
Vocal Mic Technique

OVERVIEW: Mic choice makes a big difference in the quality of the vocal sound. In the previous technique about mic choice, we saw that the most important part of the vocal tracking session was the inspired and emotional performance. Mic choice, although very important, was secondary to the quality of the performance. Mic technique, though still secondary to the inspired performance, is something that we should always strive to optimize.

CHALLENGE: Granted, world-class vocals are usually recorded using a large-diaphragm condenser mic. However, world-class vocals are usually recorded in rooms that sound great. Tracking vocals in a room that doesn't add an amazing interest to the vocal sound can be challenging. Recording vocals at home in a bedroom or family room studio can also be challenging. The mic needs to be a good choice, and the acoustical environment probably needs some treatment so that the reflections off the close surfaces don't permanently diminish the quality of the vocal sound.

SOLUTION: We previously took a look at acoustical control devices. Here's where they all truly become a requirement if your room isn't complimentary to the vocal sound:

1. The importance of acoustic treatment and portable acoustical control tools: Mic technique starts with the room. If the room sounds bad, then the mic will sound bad—I don't care how much it costs. Buying a set of foam wall panels from Acoustic Sciences or Auralex can do wonders for a room. The tool that I rely on—even in a commercial studio—is the Acoustic Sciences Corporation (ASC) Tube Trap. Surround the vocalist in almost any room with a set of eight of these devices, and your vocal track will be radically improved and probably world-class.

Used by permission. Art Noxon, Acoustic Sciences Corporation

Surround the vocalist with a set of eight ASC Tube Traps to radically improve the vocal sound—no matter what mic you're using.

2. Proximity Effect: Especially when using cardioid and bidirectional microphones, the proximity effect quickly provides an abundance of bass frequencies when the singer moves close to the microphone. However, mics with the omnidirectional pattern are not as subject to the negative influences of the proximity effect. It's important to be aware of the influences that proximity makes on any microphone. Singing close to a cardioid or bidirectional condenser mic will probably result in too much bass from the vocal unless the mic provides a high-pass filter that reduces just the right amount of low-frequency content. It's always worth trying an omnidirectional mic if the singer wants to get close to the mic because there won't be the negative influence of the proximity effect. If you want to track great-sounding vocals, then you must be aware of these variables and how they might affect the vocal sound.

3. Mic position: Once the acoustics are adequately under control, it's time to position the mic for the best sound. Usually, the mic can be placed about six inches in front of the vocalist's mouth. However, if you find that you're having problems with mouth sound, nose sounds, or if the tone isn't quite right, then try moving the mic up above the nose facing down or try moving the mic a little lower facing up. Usually, moving the mic up and facing down minimizes a nasal quality, but it all depends on the singer and the actual design of his or her vocal mechanism. Position the mic along an arc in front the vocalist to find the ideal tonal balance.

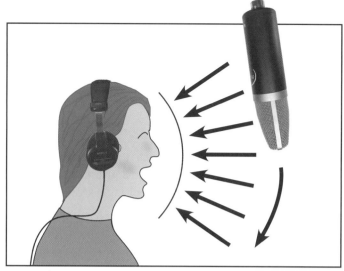

Move the mic up and down along an arc to find the best sound.

4. Gobos, baffles, and screens: Whether vocals are tracked in a small or large room, pay close attention to the intimacy of the sound and make sure it matches the musical power and emotion. Baffles, also called gobos and screens, are usually portable walls about 6–8 inches thick, 4 feet wide and 4–8 feet tall, sometimes with glass or Plexiglas in the upper portion to provide sight lines for the musicians. Baffles help shape the intimacy of the vocal sound, and they also provide isolation from other sounds being recorded in the same room as the vocals. Even though the studio might be large with a wonderful ambient sound, vocals usually need to feel more intimate and roomy, so baffles are an important tool to help achieve the appropriate sound.

5. Locating the Zone: Finding the perfect singer, microphone, room, and baffling combination might take some time and experimentation, but it's worth the effort. As the tracking engineer, you're tasked with knowing the characteristic changes that each alteration might add. Should you have the singer get close to an omnidirectional mic for a close sound without a dramatic proximity effect? Should the singer back off to a distance of a foot or so, using a cardioid condenser mic? Or should you have the singer hold a dynamic mic and use the same kind of mic technique he or she uses in a live performance? Should you use a reflection filter, a portable solution that mounts on the mic stand and absorbs some of the acoustical reflections? Each of these considerations provide a different musical feel and emotional impact. Time to start practicing!

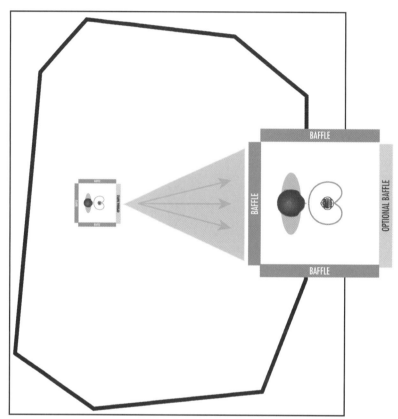

A singer surrounded by baffles in a large studio

Portable mic-stand-mounted reflection filters can be helpful.

TIP: For a dramatically intimate performance, record the vocalist in a small booth at a large studio. Use baffles to make the space even more deadened. When recording at home, try hanging blankets around and over the mic, or depending on the vocalist's claustrophobic tendencies, record the track in a closet. Most singers will do anything to make the song sound better—and everybody loves a good studio story!

TECHNIQUE 40
Backing Vocals

OVERVIEW: Backing vocals, also called background vocals, harmonies, or BGVs, are an important component in the majority of songs. They highlight the most important lyrics and add power and contrast in the production. The amount of vocals depends on the type of music and the taste of the artist and/or producer. In a rootsy rock production with an aggressive attitude, a single harmony part is the norm. Other productions might use two, three, or four separate backing parts that are tripled, quadrupled, or more!

CHALLENGE: Achieving the perfect blend of the lead vocal and BGVs is often a challenge. There are a few things the tracking engineer can do to help achieve a good vocal blend. However, it's really the singers who need to be conscious of the way their vocal sound fits with the leader and the other BGVs.

SOLUTION: The following thoughts are very helpful when tracking BGVs of all types:

1. Mic choice and vocal blend: Approach recording BGVs the same way you'd approach recording a lead vocal. Try a few mics and pick the one that sounds best on the vocalist. This is the first step in finding a good blend. Trying to choose a mic that sounds thicker or thinner is risky when guessing what the blend might need to be. You won't really know what you need in most cases until the mix comes together, so capturing a balanced and appealing sound is the safest approach. There can be an exception to that rule when recording vocal groups with an individual bass singer. Capturing a warm and full tone on the bass vocal part saves a lot of time when finding a blending tone during mixdown.

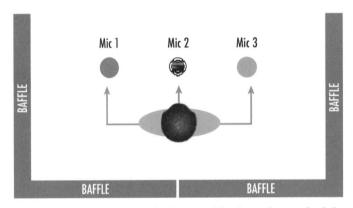

Try a few different mics on backing and lead vocalists to find the one that captures the best sound.

2. Singing together with separation: Sometimes, backing vocalists want to perform their harmonies together along with the recorded lead vocal. They might even want to track at the same time as the lead vocalist. The success of this approach depends completely on how reliable the singers are at staying in time, in tune, and in an appropriate blend. When tracking two or three singers in the same room, try using mics with a hypercardioid polar pattern because their sensitivity area is narrower than mics with a cardioid polar pattern. Have the singers stand in a line with all of the mics pointed the same direction to control the reflections and to minimize phase issues. Use baffles between the singers to increase isolation. If the singers need to see each other, then it's OK to place them in a circle. Be careful to place baffles or other absorptive material behind each singer because the reflections off the surrounding surface will dramatically decrease the vocal intimacy and cause problematic phase interactions.

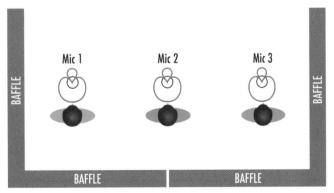

Three singers together using mics with hypercardioid patterns

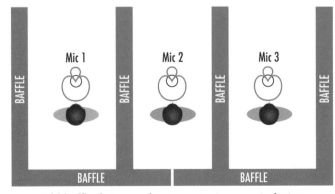

Add baffles between the singers to increase isolation.

3. Tracking one BGV: Most of the time, a single harmony is tracked as an organic-sounding part that fits well rhythmically and harmonically with the lead vocal. However, sometimes the more raw and unrefined the part, the better. Energy is the most important aspect of many single harmony parts. If the part adds to the lead vocal energy and has the same attitude, then your mission has been accomplished.

4. Multiple singers on one mic: The cleanest way to track two or three singers is to position one singer on each side of a bidirectional mic, or if there are three or more signers, gather them all around a single omnidirectional microphone. Both of these techniques capture a sound with the least amount of problematic phase interactions. However, they both rely on the singers' ability to sing in tune, in time, and with a good blend.

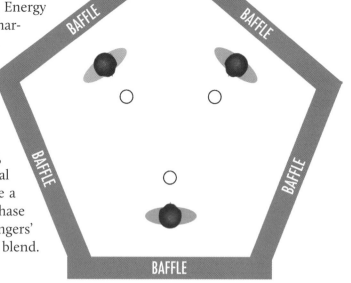

Put the vocalists in a circle so they can see each other. Use baffles behind the vocalists to control any reflection back into the mics.

5. Double and Triple Tracking: In many pop genres, double and triple tracking the BGVs as overdubs is commonplace. In the mix, panning the harmonies wide across the panorama provides an excellent contrast for the single mono lead vocal track. If the harmonies are complex, then try recording them on a couple of separate MIDI tracks and letting the singers perform their parts with a MIDI piano as a guide in the headphones. Make sure the MIDI tracks match the lead vocal's rhythm and energy. If the backing singer wants to hear the lead vocal and any additional harmonies while tracking, then provide those parts in the headphones. Just make sure the singer that's tracking hears his or her part the best. Most experienced backgound singers prefer to learn the rhythm and energy of the lead vocal and then sing the harmony along with the guide track as a reference but with very little or no other vocal parts. This approach eliminates confusion with the other parts and results in a clean and accurate track. Check after each part has been tracked to verify that they match the lead vocal and other harmonies, and then revert back to the more minimal mix. Once the performance is reliable, most engineers record two, three, four, or more of the identical parts on additional tracks. Usually, double tracking each of the backing parts provides a very impressive and wide sound, but there are techniques in mixing that can take advantage of the additional overdubs to build a variation in textures.

Tripled background vocals panned hard right, hard left, and center. When tripling vocals, it's a good idea to keep the center takes down a little in level to open up the middle for the lead vocal.

TIP: A classic technique that helps improve the vocals' blend and size involves detuning the left and right overdubs slightly. Use a tuning plug-in to raise the pitch of the left BGV overdub by 7 cents (seven 100ths of a half step). Then tune the right BGV overdub 7 cents sharp. Leave the center vocal overdubs alone. Sometimes, this technique works best without the middle harmony tracks.

TECHNIQUE 41
Vocal Groups and Choirs

OVERVIEW: From small vocal groups of four to six singers to large concert choirs, capturing the full essence of the live performance can be a challenge. Our typical goal would be to track the blend of a group of singers while also capturing the sonic interest of the acoustical environment.

CHALLENGE: Miking a choir in a live performance can be quite a challenge, especially when there are accompaniment instruments sharing the stage. Live drums and guitar amps tend to bleed into the choir mics, confusing the mix and degrading the sound of the choir and the drums. Miking a choir in a large commercial studio is much easier because of its acoustical integrity and isolation opportunities.

SOLUTION: The following techniques are very helpful when tracking vocal groups and choirs:

1. It's all about the choir: The quality of the recorded choir depends on the sound quality that the choir produces when they perform. Well, that seems like a no-brainer, right? The fact is, we're often confronted with a task that has very little chance of realizing a satisfactory conclusion. Recording a choir that produces a sound with a poor blend, problematic intonation, or the lack of a full tone or volume that embraces microphones is exactly such a task. Realistically in this case, the best tracking technique might well include a side conversation with the choir director, politely and respectfully explaining the need for the choir to produce a higher quality tone at an increased volume level.

2. Run the band direct: I know, neither of these first two techniques has anything specifically to do with mic choice, placement, processing, or mixing. However, every recording task is initially about getting everything set up for success before pressing the record button. If you're miking a choir or any vocal group that's not on individual close mics, and there are rhythm section instruments tracking at the same time, then run the instruments direct. You could also use isolation rooms for the drums, guitar amps, and any other loud source that might leak into the vocal mics. It's ideal when the vocal sound can be shaped to facilitate a blended, appealing tone and balance without leakage from the band that meets or exceeds the volume produced by the vocal group.

3. Individual mics: The decision to track with individual mics or with multiple singers per mic should be based on the style of music, the kind of vocal sound that's best for the music, the quality of the vocalists, and how many other instruments share the stage. When tracking fewer than six singers—typically more of a pop configuration—individual mics can help capture an intimate, close vocal sound. The blend can be shaped during mixdown.

4. The 3:1 Rule: Any time multiple mics are used in the same acoustical space, there's an opportunity for problematic phase combinations to diminish the sound quality. That's because the sound wave from source A reaches mics 1, 2, and 3 at different points in the wave cycle. This provides a likelihood that the combination of those mics in the mix will degrade the quality of the recorded sound due to those waves arriving at each mic during a different point in the 360-degree wave. To minimize destructive phase combinations when tracking a large sound source, adhere to the 3:1 rule, which simply states that the distance between any two microphones should be at least three times the distance from the mics to the source. Conforming to this rule helps keep the mics close enough to the source and far enough away from each other to let the intended source for each mic overwhelm destructive phase combinations.

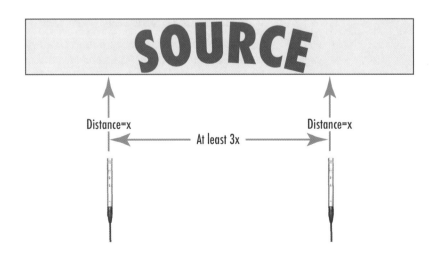

5. Traditional choir setup: Choirs are traditionally set up on risers so that each row is able to project over the top of the row in front. Some choirs use a shell design behind the choir to help reflect the sound into the venue. When miking a choir on traditional risers, take advantage of the 3:1 rule. Use three or four microphones positioned 12–18 inches in front of the first row and 12–18 inches above the top row, aimed down at the middle row. The distance between the mics needs to be at least three times the mic distance from the singers. So if the mics are 12 inches from the singers, then they should be at least 3 feet apart. Each mic will pick up between 9 and 15 singers.

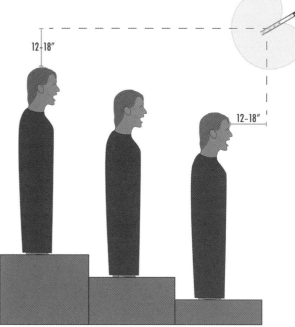

Position the mic about a foot above the top row and about a foot in front of the front row, aimed down at the middle row.

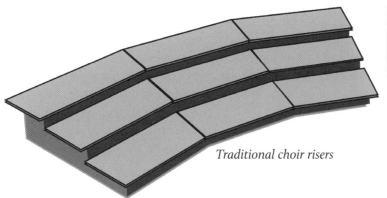

Traditional choir risers

6. Mic choice: Small-diaphragm cardioid condenser mics are preferred in most choir-miking applications. In a portable setup or when tracking in a studio, mics such as the AKG 451, AT 4041, and Neumann KM 184 are an excellent choice. When a choir is in a permanent location, such as a church or concert hall, hanging mics are preferred. Placing microphones on stands that are positioned high above the singers will eventually result in someone tripping over a cable or a mic stand, sending the mic and stand crashing to the floor. Hanging small condenser microphones from the ceiling cleans up the stage or risers and ensures that no one will knock over a mic stand. Popular hanging choir mics like the AT U853PMW are available in a wide range of prices from a variety of manufacturers.

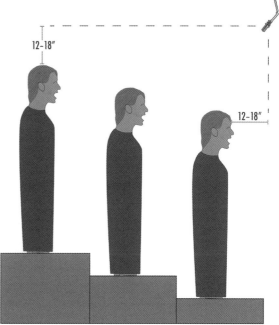

Hanging mics are positioned like any other small-diaphragm microphone, but they eliminate stands and remove clutter.

7. Choosing the number of mics to use on a choir: Any time you're tracking a large source with multiple microphones, use as few mics as possible to get the job done well. If the choir is strong with dynamic power, great intonation, and a great blend, then try a stereo mic technique like an X-Y, Blumlein, or spaced pair. Sometimes, more mics are needed to do the job well. If the music requires a closer choir sound or if isolation is important, then add more mics but adhere to the 3:1 rule to minimize problematic phase interactions.

TIP: To break away from the traditional approach to recording a choir, set up a Blumlein configuration in the middle of the room. Have the choir stand all the way around the stereo pair of mics for a great sound. Listen to Michael Jackson's "Earth Song." This is the technique Bruce Swedien used on the Andraé Crouch singers for this amazing recording.

TECHNIQUE 42
Track a Band at Home

OVERVIEW: It's one thing to track individual instruments, but tracking the entire band all at once demands an additional level of preparation and understanding about what goes into creating a great group performance. In the next set of pages, we'll assess the requirements for tracking a band at home versus tracking a band in a commercial studio. We'll also consider how to use the home and commercial studio together, getting the most out of the commercial studio and saving money by tracking at home without sacrificing quality.

CHALLENGE: The aspect of recording that most of us are missing in our home studios is a great-sounding room. So we have to make the best of what we have at our disposal. There are plenty of ways to get the most out of recording at home. It's about using the knowledge you have about capturing audio and finding ways to increase the interest of the rooms that you have available.

SOLUTION: There are several ways to get the most out of your home recordings:

1. What are the available rooms? Determine what kind of rooms will be available when you track the band. If you have a garage, than that's a great place to track the drums. It's actually best if your garage isn't finely finished with drywall and paint. Shelves with bins and gadgets make fine diffusers, as do lawnmowers and tools and all of the stuff that tends to get stored along with your cars. Closets make great isolation rooms for guitar and bass amps. Most kitchens serve as interesting live rooms, and a shower provides a wonderfully unique reverberant quality. Bedrooms are also useful as isolation rooms for amps, but they tend to be sonically the least impressive.

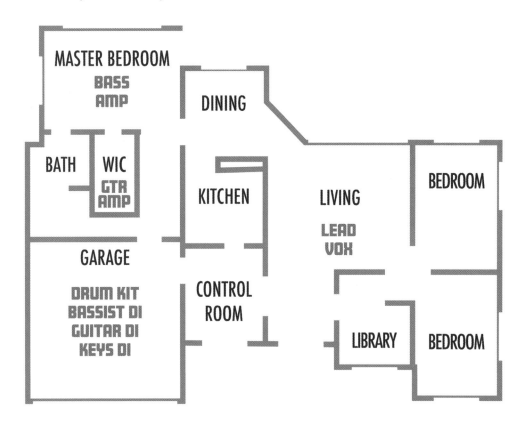

2. The first time you set up to track the band at your home, you'll probably use every cable you have on hand, connecting mics that have been run from across the house and sending headphone mixes to all of the musicians. You'll probably need to invest in additional cables, connectors, snakes, headphone amps, and so on. However, once you're functional, you'll always be able to record at home.

3. Gathering the band in one location: Notice how the drummer, guitarist, bassist, and keyboardist are all playing together in the garage while either their amps are in other rooms and/or they are connected to the recorder through a direct box. This is the same way recordings are made in most commercial studios. Typically, the drums are set up in the live room, and the rest of the musicians play from the same location with their amps set up in isolation rooms directly off the main studio. This approach is ideal because it lets the band maintain eye contact while they feed off each other's energy for the performances.

4. Setting up headphones: Most interfaces provide a couple headphone outputs that can be fed from various auxiliary (aux) and mix buses. Building a headphone system that gives the musicians enough control can be difficult. Other than the one or two outputs that the interface provides, try setting up aux buses for additional headphone sends. Most mixers provide aux outputs on the back of the mixer—this is an advantage to using a mixer as your interface. Just connect the aux output to a small headphone amplifier, and you're ready to go. You can build a mix in the aux bus for the musicians, or some digital mixers include an app that lets the musician control the headphone mix from a smartphone.

5. Interface Capacity: To efficiently record a band at home, it is necessary to have an interface with at least 16 available inputs and preferably 16 outputs. If you're using a digital mixer as your interface, than you're likely to have ample inputs and aux buses. The drums will take at least four inputs, but eight or nine inputs would be better. The bass guitar will take at least one input, but you might want to use a DI and mic the cabinet, so two channels would be better. The guitar amp requires at least one mic, and it's always a good idea to take a stereo direct feed from the guitarist's pedal board. The keyboardist will take at least two inputs for a stereo feed from the main keyboard. The vocalist will of course need an input, and you'll likely need an input for a talk-back mic. On the low side, you'll need nine mic inputs, but ideally you'll have 17 inputs ready to go. Plus, you'll need enough outputs to feed your monitors and headphones mixes. The band could theoretically share a single mix; however, that scenario is far from ideal. If you make sacrifices in the flexibility and quality of what the musicians hear, then you'll definitely sacrifice the quality of their performances. It's best if each musician has a discrete mix. For this band, there would ideally

A simple, inexpensive headphone amplifier like this PreSonus HP4 works very well when connected to a mono or stereo aux output.

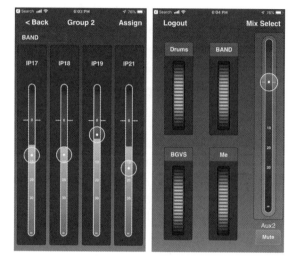

Most modern digital mixers provide an app, like this SQ4You from Allen & Heath, for the musicians to mix their own monitors.

be six separate auxiliary sends available to supply mixes to the same number of headphone amps. Also, stereo headphone mixes are much more inspiring, and they provide a listening environment that allows for more attention to detail. Therefore, six stereo headphone mixes will require 12 aux outputs.

6. Click Tracks: Some musicians and producers despise using a click track. That's especially true with young bands that thrive on the energy of unbridled tempo aggression—some might called it "rushing." That's understandable for some genres, but most of the time, it's a good idea to use a click track because it keeps the tempo stable. It also facilitates easy editing from one part of a song to another. If you need to move a harmony part from the beginning of the song to the end, then everything will fit together nicely if the band played to a click. If the band was allowed to speed up throughout the song, this kind of editing would be much more cumbersome than it should be.

7. Reference Vocals: In most tracking sessions, the lead vocal part is considered a reference vocal because it's mostly used to provide a guide to lead the rest of the band through the song. There's not enough concentration left to really focus on the vocal performance. Everyone expects that the final vocal will be performed as an overdub so that all of the energy is geared at getting the best vocal sound along with the most magical vocal performance. But, it's very important that you record the initial lead vocal like it was a final take. Make sure the levels are right and that there isn't something in the signal path that's distorting, even if the lead vocalist is just laying back on a couch in the control room and you have the monitors turned up. It's not uncommon for those first takes to be the best, probably because there is the least amount of pressure on the singer. Always record everything and keep every take.

TIP: It is most convenient if the control room monitor provides access to all of the aux sends. As the tracking engineer, it's best to listen to exactly what the musicians are hearing whenever they ask for a change. At the very least, take your headphones and plug them into the headphone amp that the musician is using to hear exactly what he or she is hearing.

TECHNIQUE 43
Tracking in a Commercial Studio

OVERVIEW: Tracking at a commercial studio is a joy! It can also be expensive, but it's fun to have assistants help set everything up, and especially fun to have them strike everything at the end. As an engineer, booking dates at a commercial studio is the best of all worlds. You're still officially in control of what happens, but you have a house engineer with another set of experiences to bounce your ideas off of. You can get a lot more done in the same time period than working in your home studio because everything is ready to go. There aren't likely to be many problems with equipment, and the house engineer will probably have already solved most problems a few different ways during previous sessions.

CHALLENGE: Some people feel the added pressure of working on the clock, which can add stress to an already stressful situation. Other people thrive in a professional environment where maintaining focus is not optional. It's worth testing the waters and booking a day in a commercial studio. You might find that the environment inspires you and the folks you work with to previously unseen heights.

SOLUTION: The following are a few recommendations to help you have a successful and exciting time in a commercial studio:

1. Learn what to expect: Visit the studio that you're interested in booking; if your area has several studios, then visit a few. The commercial studio, especially in the current era of accessible digital technology, is a customer service business. Every customer is valuable, and every successful studio knows how to make their clients feel valued and respected. So visit the studio and find out what you'll experience on the session date.

2. What's the big deal about recording in a commercial studio? There are a lot of reasons to track in a commercial studio. Primarily, they have rooms that enhance the sound of the music that's performed in them. If you really want a great drum sound, then find a room in which the

It's hard to beat the magical sounds and vibe of Capitol Studio A in Los Angeles.

drums sound great. Want a monstrous guitar sound? Find a room where the guitar sounds monstrous. The same theory holds true for strings, horns, large choirs, and most any other source that projects a substantial amount of acoustical volume. Recording in a commercial studio also commands the focus of the entire band. It's a special place where creativity can flow easily because of the environment. In the studio, lines are drawn between those who are there for technical support and those who are there to be creative. This releases a lot of burdens from those who need to be at their creative pinnacle to create great music. And, commercial studios typically have fantastic new and classic gear that is maintained well, and they're very experienced at using that gear.

3. Be prepared and well rehearsed: Preproduction is even more important when you're renting a studio. When you're working at home, moving at a relaxed pace is OK, but if you're like most people, then you want to squeeze every ounce of value out of your hard-earned money. You'll want to be sure to have as many details as possible covered in advance of the session.

4. Plan out the tracks you'll need in advance: This step is an excellent organizational exercise because it forces you to visualize exactly how you see the session unfolding. The studio will probably want a track list anyway, so map out exactly what tracks you'll need along with preferred microphones where appropriate.

Artist: The Brain Hogs			
Engineer: Bill Gibson			
NUMBER	TRACK NAME	MICROPHONE	NOTES
1	Hat	KM84	Pad on
2	Kick IN	Beat 52	Aim at beater
3	Kick OUT	U 47 fet	Close left
4	SubKick	LoFrEQ	Close right
5	Snare TOP	Beta 56	
6	Snare BOTTOM	421	Set roll-off to "S"
7	Rack Tom	414 XLII	Pad -18, 80 HZ cut
8	Floor Tom	414 XLII	Pad -18, 80 HZ cut
9	OH Ride side	Royer 122	Pad on
10	OH Hat side	Royer 122	Pad on
11	Room Ride side	M50	
12	Rom Hat side	M50	
13	Ride	451	Pad -20, 150 Hz cut

Plan ahead! Send a list of tracks along with the microphones you prefer to use to the studio before the session.

5. Create guide tracks with click and reference parts: When preparing for the studio date, finalize the tempo, key, and feel for each song. As part of preparation and preproduction, record a reference version of each song with a guide vocal, click track, reference groove, and possibly reference pads or synth parts. Add anything to the reference recording that you imagine will be helpful. If you are hiring studio musicians to augment the band, then it's helpful to record one track where someone says the number of each measure relative to the chart all the way through the song. If your home DAW is the same one used at the studio you're booking, just save

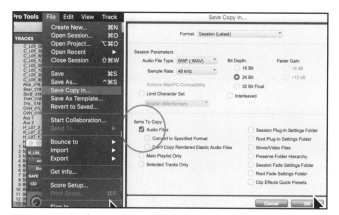

Be sure to check that box to include the audio in the copy you make to take to the session.

a version of the file that also saves the audio WAV or AIFF files. Most DAWs provide a means to make a traveling copy of your files. Pro Tools calls the copy that regenerates all audio files into the same folder "Save Copy In..." Logic uses the terms "Consolidate" and "Project Package." Just make sure that the box is checked to save the audio with the file. Sometimes, audio files are accessed where they reside without actually being copied into the project. It's important to make sure all files are copied into the traveling folder so you don't show up at a session with half of your audio files missing. If your DAW lacks the ability to package all of the files up into one clean file, then simply bounce all of the tracks out as contiguous files that start at the beginning of the sequence and generate through the end of the session. Some DAWs call this process a "bounce;" others might call it a "freeze" or "consolidation." Others might simply require that the session folder is copied because all audio is automatically copied into that folder.

6. Trust the house engineer: Once the session date arrives and you're setting the band up, feel free to rely on the house engineer. He or she has probably done several sessions similar to yours, and therefore will have valuable insights about what will get the best results.

7. To use analog tape or not to use analog tape: If the studio has an analog multitrack recorder, you'll need to decide whether to use it or not. Personally, I love the sound of drums tracked on a great analog multitrack. However, there is a point of diminishing returns because it takes longer to use the analog recorder. First, the reason you'd want to use the analog recorder would be to capture the sound of pushing the recording levels to tape and the natural and warm compression this process offers. But, once each take is done, all of the files need to be recorded back into the DAW in order to keep the cleanest version of the recording—analog tape loses high end over time. In addition to the time it takes to transfer the audio back into the DAW, recording while locked to an analog recorder is much slower than simply using a DAW. Getting the sequence from bar 100 to bar 10 is just a few key strikes away—it's virtually instantaneous. But, in the analog domain, that same move could involve 20 or 30 seconds, and then you would just end up in the vicinity of the 10-second mark. Most engineers feel that recording the entire session at 96-kHz/24-bit or 192-kHz/24-bit captures audio quality that matches or exceeds the personality that analog tape adds to the session. Therefore, bypassing the analog step has become very common, even at the top where the highest quality work is demanded.

8. The vibe is still important in the commercial studio, so do whatever you need to do in order to set the perfect mood for each song: Above all, make sure that you get everything right. One great recorded song has value. Ten poorly executed productions have no value at all.

TIP: Record room mics to separate tracks anytime it's possible. The personality that a great-sounding studio adds to any recording has great value. For any instrument that's being recorded in the big rooms, set up and track a stereo pair of room mics. Whenever possible, track a pair of room mics close to the source and a pair that is far away and up high.

TECHNIQUE 44
Commercial and Home Studio

OVERVIEW: Prior to the start of the '90s, commercial studios were essential to the entire recording process. Through the mid- to late-'80s, home studios were popping up around the country. However, they were really just smaller versions of commercial studio with limited space but much of the same gear as most commercial studios. Digital options were prohibitively expensive with the recorder of the day costing $120,000—an AMS AudioFile two-track monochrome digital recorder with no waveform view. But at the turn of the '90s, we found Digital Performer from MOTU, the Alesis ADAT, and Digidesign lining up with several products, including Pro Tools. All of these conditions unleashed an era where virtually anyone could record, edit, and mix first-class digital audio at home. It was an amazing development—one that hit commercial studios incredibly hard.

CHALLENGE: Commercial studios were most severely impacted with the development and release of many new digital tools. It started to get ugly for a while, because even though the studios tried to fight back, they were fighting a losing battle. The genie was out of the bottle, so to speak. Equilibrium took a while, but the industry has settled into a mode that values everything about the commercial studio yet understands that some things are more efficient to work on at home.

SOLUTION: If you want to get the most from your recordings, then combine the best of the commercial studio with the things you like best about working at home.

1. Whom, What, Where, When, and Why: It all comes down to figuring out *why* you want *what* to be recorded *when*, *where*, and by *whom*. In other words, answer the question, "What makes the most sense and gets the best results?"

2. Drums in the big house: I like to plan sessions in the studio around the drums. It's great for feel, passion, and energy to have the entire band at a session in a commercial studio. However, when it comes time to focus, I pay closest attention to the drums simply because I don't have a big enough room in my home studio to get the most out of a drum kit. If all I walked out of the session with were great drum takes on all of the tunes I planned on recording, then I'd consider that a win. The fact that there might have been several other tracks that captured awesomely inspired and great-sounding performances is frosting on my drum cake. So decide which tracks are most important to capture at the studio and focus primarily on those—don't let other tracks slow you down.

Tracking in a commercial studio is always an amazing experience—and it gets you out of your cave! I highly recommend it.

3. Other big room instruments: Essentially, every instrument that puts out a lot of sound can benefit from a great-sounding room. So in addition to drums being a wise choice to record in the commercial studio, electric guitars, brass instruments and sections, stringed instruments and sections, grand piano, percussion instruments, and so on, can also benefit from the rooms in a traditional studio.

4. Back for more: Devise your ideal strategy before recording a note. Imagine contingencies and establish the non-negotiable items on your list. If your project has a full band, a five-piece horn section, and a 30-voice gospel choir, then your strategy is dictated already—it really is usually this easy. Drums need the big room, but you could get by recording the drums in your garage. However, the horns need the space for the sound to develop, and reflections coming back from any surface closer than 5 or 10 feet will seriously damage the recorded sound. And, you would not be doing justice to a 30-voice gospel choir by tracking them in a family room or a garage. OK, I confess: I've done all three of the previous things—actually in my home studio and in a commercial studio. That's how I can say with confidence, "Save your pennies and book a great studio for tracking these and other loud sources!"

5. Bring the project home to track vocals… or not: Realistically, 99 percent of all lead and backing vocal tracks turn out better when you record them in your home studio because singers are mental beings. They need to feel comfortable, and pressure is a killer when it comes to creating an emotional vibe. The pressure of being on the clock at a commercial facility can be a problem for most singers. But—and this is a big "but"—some singers just have to know that they're in the best studio on the planet to do their best work. Anything else won't do. If your singer is like that, put it on your list of non-negotiables that the lead vocal needs to be recorded at a commercial studio. Don't fight it. The singer won't be convinced about how much more relaxed it is to record in your home studio or how your signal path is identical to the one in the commercial studio. They need to feel like they're performing in the best place possible. I said it before—singers are mental beings. Their instrument is themselves. An hour or so per song spent at an extra-fancy commercial recording studio is absolutely nothing if what they provide is a hit performance!

6. Mix at home: It is usually best to do your mixing at home because you can spend the time it takes to get it right. The only problem with that approach is that, no matter what, you'll spend the time it takes to get it right. Any time you're in that situation, you're likely to succumb to "the paralysis of analysis." You'll never finish! Realize this: The deadline is your friend! It forces us to get things done. When I'm producing a project, I always ask for the "drop dead" date (the final "It's gotta be done" date). Then, I schedule the mastering session with a great mastering engineer who is very busy, and would have a problem with me canceling. That deadline needs to consider any time that's needed between the completion of mastering and the delivery of the final product. That provides a hard deadline that I'm unlikely to miss.

Record the parts that require space and lots of gear at a commercial studio. Then take the project to your home studio for overdubs and mixdown. Transporting a project between a commercial studio and the home studio is a very common approach to music creation.

TIP: Transport your session files to the commercial studio on a hard drive or thumb drive. Copy the files onto the studio computer system to take advantage of the stability of their setup. At the end of the session, copy the new session files back onto your drive to transport to your home studio. An added benefit to this routine is that the studio then has a backup of your session to that date.

OVERVIEW: Compressors are important tools in the recording chain. Some engineers use them a lot, and other more purist engineers use them a little. When recording in the analog domain, compressors are used during tracking in order to get a hotter signal printed to tape, which helps hide the noise floor. In the digital realm, compressors are used for their sonic quality and to establish a dynamic position for various mix ingredients. The majority of tracking to a DAW doesn't require the use of compression for the sake of dynamic control. However, tracking something like a vocal or bass guitar through a high-quality outboard preamp/compressor can add an appealing warmth to the sound that's hard to beat in the DAW. Compressors, gates, and other dynamics processors have become mostly mixing tools when using a DAW, but there are situations where they are either a good idea or necessary to use during a tracking session.

CHALLENGE: Whenever used too aggressively, compressors can quickly remove too much of the dynamic content that gives music its energy and excitement. That's why some of the best engineers such as Bruce Swedien (Michael Jackson, Quincy Jones, and many more) and Al Schmitt (Paul McCartney, Diana Krall, and others) use as little compression as they possibly can. Our challenge is to take advantage of the benefits of compression without overdoing it while not being afraid to use the amount of compression required to successfully get the job done.

SOLUTION: If you understand how to use dynamics processors, you'll be able to include them skillfully in your work for excellent results.

1. What is compression? The compressor is an automatic volume control triggered to turn down by the amount of energy (**amplitude**) generated by the incoming audio signal. There is an amplifier in the circuit that turns down the level in correlation to the incoming voltage, the source of which is the increasing and decreasing amplitude of the audio wave. An increase in audio level is seen by the amplifier as an increase in voltage. If everything is set up correctly, then every time the voltage exceeds a strength level called the "threshold," which you select, the amplifier turns the audio level down. Once the voltage decreases below the threshold, the amplifier regains its original full-on state. This level variance is controlled by the VCA.

2. The real result from compression: A compressor compresses the dynamic range into a smaller package, automatically turning down the loudest parts of an audio track. However, the actual result of compression isn't a decrease in the loudest portions, because part of the setup routine on a compressor involves regaining the overall level lost by the automatic reduction of the volume peaks. So if the gain was reduced by 6 dB and then the level was increased by 6 dB to bring the peak level back to normal, then the actual result is that the quiet portions increase 6 dB in level with the peak level the same as it was prior to compression.

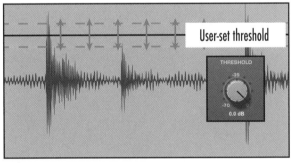

Move the threshold up and down with the threshold control. Voltage that's above the threshold will be acted on. Voltage below it will not.

3. Threshold: The threshold is set by the user. Signal voltage that's below the threshold is not acted upon by the VCA. Signal voltage that's above the threshold is turned down according to the settings of the device parameters.

4. Ratio: The ratio—expressed as a mathematical ratio such as 2:1, 3:1, 4:1, and so on—determines what happens to the portion of the signal that exceeds the threshold. If the ratio is set at 2:1, it simply means that, for every 2 dB that exceeds the threshold, the VCA will only allow 1 dB to exceed the threshold. So, if the signal exceeds the threshold by 8 dB, the VCA turns down and the resulting signal would only exceed the threshold by 4 dB. Likewise, with a ratio of 4:1, a signal that exceeds the threshold by 12 dB would only surpass the threshold by 3 dB for a gain reduction of 9 dB.

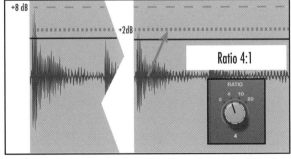

With a ratio of 4:1, the +8 dB peak (dashed line) is reduced to a +2 dB peak (dotted line) for a gain reduction of 6 dB.

5. **Attack:** The attack time control determines the time delay between the exact time that the signal exceeds the threshold and the exact time that the VCA acts to turn the signal down. Set the attack to the fastest setting—usually a fraction of a millisecond—to compress the transient along with the body of the tone. Slow the attack time down to let the transient pass through unaffected while compressing the body of the notes. For example, it's common on drums to set the attack time slow (between about 10 and 30 ms) to accentuate the attack but also to warm up the ringing tone of the snare, toms, or kick.

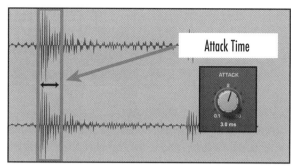

Lengthen the attack time to accentuate the transient attack. Shorten the attack time to compress all or a smaller part of the transient attack.

6. **Release:** The release time determines how long it takes the VCA to turn back up once the signal goes back below the threshold after compressing the audio. This is an important parameter because it can help elongate or accentuate the tone of the sounds. It's important that the release time is long enough to ramp back up in a way that positively affects the sound. However, it shouldn't be so long that it never lets the level return to normal before needing to compress the next note. You should be able to watch the gain reduction meter and see it turning down and then back up again, basically in time with the music.

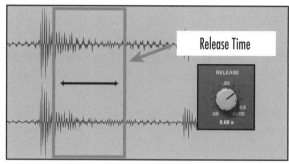

Set the release time to control the body of the tone that happens after the attack.

7. **Gain Reduction (GR):** When discussing a compressor and what it's doing to the audio passing through it, gain reduction is a critical specification. You can have everything set up by the book, but if there is no reading on the gain reduction meter, then the compressor isn't doing anything. Setting up the compressor is about deciding where you want the controls set and then adjusting the threshold for the desired gain reduction. There are a few types of meters that show how much the gain is being reduced, but the two most common are: 1) The backwards VU meter starts at 0 VU (no GR) and moves to the left to register GR. 2) The backwards dBFS meter moves from the top down to register GR.

8. **Knee:** The **knee** parameter softens the action of establishing gain reduction once the audio signal passes the threshold. With the knee set to zero, the VCA turns the signal above the threshold down according to all of the rest of the settings as soon as the signal exceeds the threshold. However, slowing the knee down causes the VCA to gently reduce the gain over a range of several dB.

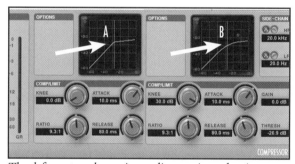

The left meter shows immediate gain reduction once the signal exceeds the threshold (A). The right meter shows a soft knee where the VCA slowly engages the compressor (B).

> **TIP:** The controls are pretty close to identical on every compressor with some occasional exceptions, but not all compressors are sonically identical. They each bring an individual personality to your tracks. Test them out and listen closely. Compressors modeled after classic hardware are very close to the originals, and they offer a lot of character for your tracks.

TECHNIQUE 46
Using the Compressor

OVERVIEW: Because compressors are such versatile processors, there are several different functions they can perform. The basic function is exactly what the name of this device says: it compresses the dynamic range of an audio wave into a tighter dynamic range.

CHALLENGE: When used skillfully, it's hard to tell when the compressor is actually compressing the dynamic range—even when checking before and after versions. Add to that the fact that the best compressors make it even more difficult to hear when compression is happening. You might find yourself frustrated and insecure about what, if anything, the compressor is doing.

SOLUTION: If you follow a routine procedure setting up the compressor, then you'll know for sure what the compressor is doing, and you'll be able to quickly know how extreme the compression is. Once you are sure of what it's doing, you'll get better at hearing what it's doing. Then you'll be able to set the device to over-compress the audio to the point that your ear will know exactly what to listen for. When audio is compressed too much, it sounds small and starts to lose its impact and life. The goal is to compress the track just enough to control the loud passages so that the quiet passages are more aurally visible in the mix. However, the fact that even a great compressor removes some of the natural acoustic life from the sound source explains why many of the all-time best and iconic engineers only use compression minimally. However, other equally awesome and iconic engineers aren't bashful about using a lot of compression when it suits the needs of the music they're mixing. It's a beautiful tool that each individual tracking and mixing engineer has the creative freedom to use to fulfill the vision they have for the music at hand. I guess that's why they call the creation of music an art! Follow the setup routine below when you're adjusting a compressor, and you'll always be able to determine and detect exactly what the compressor is doing.

1. Compression versus limiting: A compressor and a **limiter** are really the same device being used in two different ways, all depending on the ratio setting. Compression uses ratio settings below 10:1. Limiters use a ratio of 10:1 and above. Functionally, a compressor decreases the overall dynamic range of the complete amplitude range. The limiter, on the other hand, typically keeps everything below the threshold intact and primarily limits everything above the threshold to a much tighter dynamic range. Limiters tend to use a fast attack time so that the VCA acts instantaneously on signals that exceed the threshold, whereas compressors tend to use slower attack times to avoid taking the life out of transients and **sibilance** (the harsh sounds produced by certain consonants).

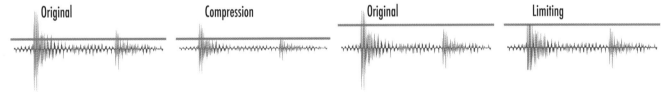

| Original | Compression | Original | Limiting |

Notice (above) that compression decreases the dynamic range, but there is still amplitude above the threshold. With limiting, the threshold is higher, but there is no amplitude above the threshold. This is the functional difference between a compressor and limiter even though the controls provide ample latitude to let the user create many hybrids of either.

2. Set the ratio: The ratio control establishes specifically what the compressor is doing. The rest of the controls establish specifically how the compressor accomplishes the mission you prescribe by the ratio setting. Therefore, this is the first thing that should be determined. There is time for fine-tuning all of the settings later, and the ratio setting might be one of the adjustments that you'll want to make. The ratio control can be set across a very wide range from 1:1, which results in absolutely no compression regardless of where the other controls are set, to ∞:1, which simply won't let anything above the threshold when the attack time is set to its fastest setting. Recommended ratio settings for compression are 2:1 to 7:1. Recommended ratio settings for limiting are 10:1 to ∞:1. Whether compressing or limiting, it's up to the engineer to decide if the waves just need to be compressed into a tighter dynamic range or if most of the amplitude should be left alone with just the peaks above the threshold affected.

Compression uses a ratio below 10:1. Limiting uses a ratio from 10:1 to ∞:1.

3. Set the attack time: The attack time setting is very critical. Since this controls how long it takes for the VCA to engage once the signal exceeds the threshold, the user chooses whether or not to let the transient attack pass through unaffected, or if the compressor will act immediately on the initial attacks. When compressing most sources, lengthening the attack time helps retain the original dynamic life by keeping the transients and/or sibilance. As a starting point, set the attack time to 10–20 ms when compressing most sources. This is a setting that you can fine-tune as the sound comes together. If the source is being limited, leaving most of the signal unprocessed and limiting the transient content, then start with the attack time at its fastest setting usually measured in **microseconds** (thousandths of a millisecond).

4. Set the release time: The release time needs to be set fast enough so that the VCA has time to release the level back to full strength before the next note needs to be compressed. If you know the tempo of the song and background unit of the fastest commonly played notes, then it's possible to calculate the spaces between the notes using the formula 60,000 divided by **BPM** (beats per minute), which equals the length in milliseconds of the quarter note. So, if the tempo is 120 BPM, then the length of each eighth note is 250 ms (60,000÷120=500 ms per quarter note or 250 ms per eighth note). This is good information, but no matter what the math says, use your eyes and ears to fine-tune the release setting. Watch the meter; if it's moving in time with the beat and you can see that it recovers in time for the VCA to react to the next note—and it sounds natural—then you're set. It doesn't necessarily need to recover for the fastest notes, but it should recover for the primary rhythmic background unit (usually eighth notes).

5. Check the input level: Once you've set the ratio, attack time, and release time, set the input level on the hottest part of the track to avoid clipping and to leave a few dB of headroom.

6. Adjust the threshold for the desired amount of gain reduction: This is the setting that lets you see how much the compressor is affecting the signal. Adjust the threshold so that you see some gain reduction, and then keep adjusting the threshold until the meter reads your desired amount of gain reductions. When tracking or mixing most vocals and instruments, the gain reduction should be somewhere between about 3 and 6 dB during the loudest passages. However, it's also very important that there are times when there is no gain reduction. If there is always gain reduction, the compressor circuit is engaged all the time, which will cause the sound quality to be substantially degraded.

7. Fine tune the ratio, attack time, and release time to achieve the sound that best fits the music: This is the point where the setting can be refined to capture the most musical sound. Adjust the attack time to let the desired amount of transient pass through. This adjustment will affect the amount of gain reduction. With the attack time on its fastest setting, you will see the most gain reduction because it will be compressing the transient, which is up to about 9 dB above the average level. Evaluate the release time to confirm that it is recovering in time for the VCA to respond to the primary beats. As you listen, move the ratio a little higher and lower to adjust for the best sound.

8. Set the makeup gain control so that the output level matches the input level: Once all of the settings are adjusted, check the output level to confirm that it matches the input level. Recheck the input level and compare it to the output level to make sure the input is still set correctly and that any gain that was lost in the compression process is regained.

Summary of compressor setup routine. 1) Ratio 2) Attack 3) Release 4) Input Level 5) Threshold 6) Makeup gain 7) Match peak output level to peak input level

TIP: Many compressors provide a mix control that lets you sweep between wet and dry. The wet setting is the 100-percent compressed signal—as if there weren't a mix control. The dry setting provides the original signal with no compression. Try setting up extreme compression with a fast attack time and blending between wet and dry for a natural sound with increased intimacy.

TECHNIQUE 47
Compressing Vocals and Instruments

OVERVIEW: Once you understand the parameters accessible in the compressor and how to set them up, then you should find it relatively easy to start trying out compressors in your tracking and mixing experiences. In this section, we'll see some common settings for vocals, drums, and electric and acoustic guitars.

CHALLENGE: The compressor is a vastly flexible device, which simply means that you need to figure out what you want it to do before you start twiddling the knobs and buttons, whether they're knobs on hardware or virtual plug-in controls.

SOLUTION: Practice listening closely while you adjust the parameters. This section provides starting points for some basic compression tasks:

1. Vocal ratio: Each singer is unique, so it's impossible to have a single go-to setup. However, there is a pretty consistent range of settings for compressing a vocalist. Assess the singer and determine if they are explosive or if they sing at a relatively constant volume that would call for pretty gentle compression with a low ratio around 3:1. With an explosive vocalist, compress with a higher ratio, between about 5:1 and 10:1, which is more like limiting. Set the threshold so that only the loudest parts of the track exceed the threshold. The higher ratio will severely decrease the amount that the processed signal exceeds the threshold.

2. Vocal attack: The attack time on a vocal track needs to be long enough to avoid eliminating the sibilant sounds and transients, but not so long that they become exaggerated. Usually, an attack time between 10 and 50 ms works well. However, if you look at the waveform and highlight an "s" in a lyric line, then you'll quickly see that an "s" can easily be 100 ms long or more. The way the sound hits the input and the setting of the threshold, really determines how much the sound will drive the compressor circuit. If the attack time is too short, then sibilant sounds like "s" will lose the attack and turn into "th" sounds.

Notice the highlighted "s" in the lyrics. In the counter window, the start, end, and length of the highlighted region show that this "s" is 114 ms long.

3. Vocal release: The release time on a vocal track is usually between about 100 and 500 ms. Watch the gain reduction meter while the track plays to see how the releases are matching the notes in the vocal part. The exact release time setting depends on the tempo, the fastest notes, and the overall sound of the part.

4. Vocal input and gain reduction: Adjust the input level for a moderate level, leaving enough headroom for the increase that tends to happen during the vocal performance. Then, adjust the threshold for a maximum gain reduction of about 6 dB. To keep the compressed sound as clean and natural as possible, it's very important that there are some passages during the vocal track that don't register gain reduction.

5. Drum Ratio: The function of compression on the kick, snare, and toms is ordinarily the same—to make the hits more consistent in volume, to accentuate the attack, and augment the tone. The ratio control is usually set between about 3:1 and 7:1.

6. Drum attack and release: On the kick, snare, and toms, the attack setting is used to accentuate the transient caused when the stick hits the drum. An attack time between 10 and 50 ms is typical, but everything depends on the drum, the stick being used, the drummer, and the desired sound. To find the best attack time setting, start with the attack at its fastest setting and slowly increase the attack time until the attack has the impact that fits with the song's intensity. Adjust the release time to elongate the tone portion of the snare, tom, or kick.

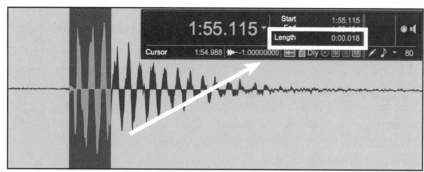

The highlighted portion of this snare drum hit is the attack, at the onset of the snare sound and just before the body of the snare tone. Notice in the counter window that the length of the highlighted region is 18 ms.

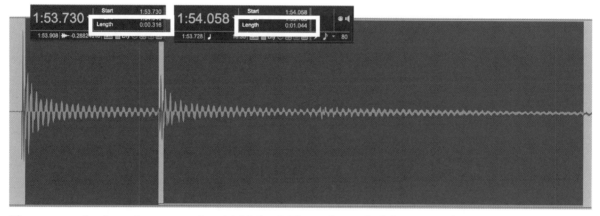

These tom strokes have the tone portions highlighted. The stroke on the left is 318 ms long, and the next hit rings for 1.044 seconds. It depends on the tempo, but release times for toms tend to be between 250 ms and 1 second.

7. Drum overheads: Whether or not the overheads on the drumset are compressed depends on the genre and the type of drum sound. Often, overheads are compressed to smooth out the overall sound and to blend the drum sounds together, especially when the kick, snare, and toms are close-miked and very clean. When compressing the overheads and accentuating the attacks, it's typical to set the ratio around 4:1 and the attack time between 20 and 40 ms. Sometimes limiting the overheads is appropriate to really blend everything together, using a fast attack time and a ratio above 10:1.

8. Electric Guitar: Electric guitarists almost always carry their own effects with them, including compression, so it isn't usually necessary to add more compression unless the guitar needs it later during mixdown. When the electric guitar sound is recorded directly into the mixer without any effects, assess its needs and either compress it to bring out the attack or limit it to smooth out the level.

9. Acoustic Guitar: The steel-string acoustic guitar has a wide dynamic range and typically requires compression to stay in the same range for mixdown. It's usually helpful to accentuate the attack on acoustic guitar so that it can stand out better in the mix without excessively boosting the level or hyping the high-frequency band. The ratio setting on acoustic is usually between 3:1 and 7:1. A typical attack time is 10–20 ms. Typical release times are 100–500 ms depending on the musical part, with 3–6 dB of gain reduction.

> **TIP:** Parallel compression takes advantage of mild compression along with limiting. For example, try applying mild compression to your entire drum mix sub-group, then routing that mix to a separate stereo aux channel. Limit the new aux channel heavily, and then turn it up just enough to add more excitement and blend to the drum mix.

TECHNIQUE 48
Gates and Expanders

OVERVIEW: Gates and expanders are identical to compressors and limiters in that they use a VCA to vary the signal in response to changes in voltage. However, whereas compressors and limiters turn the signal above the threshold down relative to the ratio control, gates and expanders turn the signal below the threshold down relative the range control.

CHALLENGE: Ideally, the proper use of compression and limiting will not be immediately detectable by the listener because those processes focus on dynamic control of primarily the loudest passages. Gates and expanders, on the other hand, are most frequently being used to clean up tracks by turning down leakage, hums, and buzzes. The settings aren't always easy to configure so that the process is unnoticeable. Frequently, the threshold, attack, release, and range controls must be precisely set, or they can cause more problems than they solve. With that said, gates and expanders are very useful tools when used expertly and creatively.

SOLUTION: It's important to be familiar with the controls on gates and expanders. It's also important to practice implementing these valuable tools so that, when needed, you can take advantage of the powerful controls they offer.

1. Threshold: The threshold control on a gate is like the threshold on a compressor, except that, while the compressor turns everything above the threshold down according to the ratio setting, the gate turns everything below the threshold down by an amount determined by the range control. The adjustment of the threshold is fundamentally important to the way the VCA can respond to incoming signals. It must be set so that all intended signals open the gate while not allowing unintended signals to open the gate. For example, gating snare and tom tracks can be difficult because there

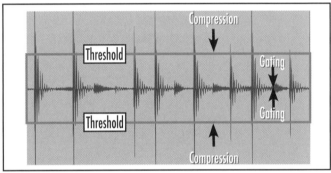

A compressor turns down the signal that exceeds the threshold, but a gate turns down the signal below the threshold.

is always a lot of leakage between the tom and snare mics; there might not be a large enough difference between the tom hits and the snare leakage to make gating a simple matter.

2. Attack: The attack time setting simply controls how quickly the VCA releases the signal once it exceeds the threshold. In other words, it controls how quickly the closed gate opens in response to strong signals. For instruments such as drums and percussion, or any other instrument where the transient is an important part of the sound, the attack time should be as fast as possible to avoid decreasing the impact from the transient. The attack time can also be used to intentionally soften entrances with settings that range from a few microseconds to a few hundred milliseconds.

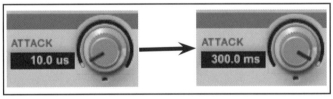

Use fast attack times for percussion instruments and slow attack times for added control over instruments like strings that often have very soft attacks.

3. Look Ahead: The "look ahead" parameter does exactly what it says. It keeps an eye on what's coming up so the VCA can react immediately to transients. This actually lets the user slow down the attack time just a little to help avoid clicks that can be heard when the super-fast attack time opens the gate. Or, it just warns the gate to be ready for a transient so that the quick attack time sounds both natural and energetic.

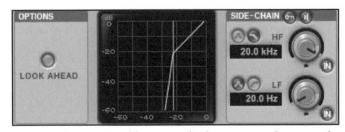

Modern plug-ins are able to see what's coming and prepare the circuit to respond to fast transients instantly without annoying pops or clicks.

4. Filters: Many gates provide high- and low-pass filters, which help the user fine-tune the way the device responds to incoming signals.

5. Release: The release time controls the length of time before the VCA turns down once the signal passes back below the threshold, typically ranging from a few milliseconds to several seconds. With the attack and release times adjusted to their fastest settings, the gate snaps open and shut as the signal rises above and below the threshold, which is unnatural for most sounds. Adjust the release time to follow the natural envelope of the source sound up and down for the most appealing sound.

6. Hold: The hold control lets the user define the length of time delay before the gate turns down once the signal passes back below the threshold. The hold control is helpful when setting up a gate for a difficult source with troublesome leakage. On a few gate/expanders that emulate classic Neve channel strips, a **hysteresis** control is provided that is similar to the hold control.

7. Range: There are several dynamics processors that perform both compression and gating tasks using the same controls. Attack, release, and threshold controls are common to both devices but the ratio control on the compressor becomes the range control on the gate. Whereas the ratio control measures the severity of gain reduction above the threshold, the range control simply determines the amount, in dBs, that the signal below the threshold is attenuated. Most range controls sweep from 0 dB to at least -40 dB, or even -80 dB, or -∞, so there is quite a wide range of available attenuation.

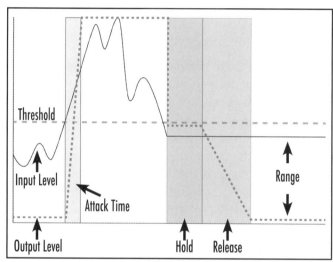

The gate/expander reacts predictably according to settings of the threshold, attack, hold, release, and range controls.

8. The difference between a gate and an expander: Virtually all gates are also expanders. Both devices have the same controls, so it can be confusing when trying to understand the difference. However, the difference is very similar to the difference between a compressor with a ratio below 10:1 and a limiter, which has a ratio of 10:1 and above. Think of a gate as closing off the signal the same way a fence gate slams shut, with the range set for a maximum cut. Think of an **expander** as a device that increases dynamic range (expands it) by turning the quiet parts down a little, with a more gentle cut of a few

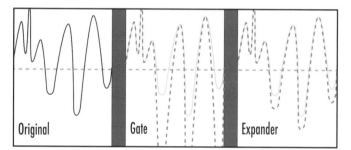

A gate turns everything below the threshold off. An expander turns everything below the threshold down according to the range control.

dB via the range control. Gates are very good at getting rid of buzzes and noise on sources such as electric guitars and basses. They don't change the noise level when the gate is open—the noises are often masked then by the loud guitar anyway—but when the instrument stops playing, the gate closes off the signal to complete silence. Expanders are very good at making simple changes to the dynamic range of a source. For example, tom tracks within a drum kit capture a lot of the rest of the kit, which can be helpful to the overall sound. Using a gate and closing them off completely between tom hits can be a problem because when the gate opens, the sound changes noticeably. However, an expander can turn the tom tracks down just a few dB to clean up the drum sound a little between hits while maintaining a consistent sound throughout the track.

TIP: Virtually all gates and expanders provide an external input, also called a "key" input, which directs the VCA to be triggered by an alternate source rather than the source being gated. Try running a brassy synth sound through the gate while connecting the output of a click or hi-hat eighth-note pattern to the key input. Press the key button and hear the synth playing the hi-hat/click pattern!

Delays

OVERVIEW: Delays are important in the recording process. They're often thought of as the echo off canyon walls that bounce back and forth a few times before they dissipate away. They definitely are that, but they're so much more. Short delays of just a few milliseconds can create a range of creative effects, especially when they are varied slightly faster or slower over time.

CHALLENGE: Finding a way to use delays to enhance the source sound rather than confusing the source is usually the goal. However, there are several useful techniques that artfully use delays to create a mix with a very musical blend.

SOLUTION: Understanding the different types of delays and how they can help bring new life and energy to your music is fundamentally important:

1. Slapback: In its simplest form, a **slapback** is a single delayed playback of the source sound. The brain acknowledges this single delay as a strong reflection off a distant wall or surface, hence, interpreting that delay as an indicator of the size of the acoustical space the listener is in. Since sound travels at a little over one foot per millisecond (1.126 ft/ms), a 338 ms slapback delay would indicate that the room is roughly 150 feet long—150 feet to the far wall and back. This simple slapback delay is enough to add size and dimension to any track.

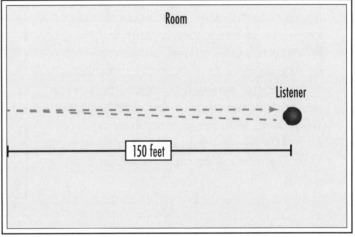

Sound travels at about 1126 feet per second (about 1.126 feet per millisecond). So the time it takes for sound to travel 150 feet away and back is about 300 (feet) times 1.126, or 338 ms.

$$60{,}000 \div \text{BPM} = \text{♩ (ms)}$$

2. Conforming to a tempo: In the context of a song or production, the slapback delay is often calculated so that it relates to the song tempo, frequently as an eighth- or quarter-note value, but also often as a quarter-note triplet or even a dotted eighth note. A delay that's randomly set in a song can be distracting and rhythmically confusing. However, a delay that's in time with the music supports the groove and rhythmic feel. A simple Google search for "delay to BPM note value" results in delay-length tables that automatically calculate the note durations relative to tempo. But, I've found that it's quicker and more efficient to simply do the calculation, either using head calculations or the calculator app on a device or computer. It's really very simple. Since there are 1000 milliseconds in a second and 60 seconds in a minute, there are 60,000 ms per minute. If you know the beats per minute (BPM) of the music, it's a simple step to realize that 60,000 divided by the BPM results in the number of milliseconds per quarter note. Once the quarter-note length has been calculated, simply divide the results by two for the eighth note, four for the sixteenth note, three for the triplet, and so on.

3. Regeneration: A single slapback delay quite effectively defines the size of the simulated acoustical environment. However, **regeneration**—a process that delays the delayed signal again and again—is frequently applied to the slapback. You can use multiple regenerated slapback delays to help blend the source track into the mix.

4. Leave the source track in place: When using a delay, it's almost always best to leave the source channel dry and clean, routing a split from the source channel to the delay device and bringing the 100-percent delay channel(s) back into the mixer on separate returns or mixer channels.

5. EQ: In the analog era, slapback delays were created using a two-track tape recorder. The signal was sent to the tape recorder input and recorded, but the playback was set to monitor from the playback head, which was spaced just far enough from the record head to cause a delay. The exact delay depended on the tape speed. The delay length doubled each time the tape speed was cut in half, from 30 to 15 to 7.5 inches per second (ips). Regeneration could be created by feeding the delayed signal coming from the playback head back into the record head again. In the analog world, each tape regeneration lost high-frequency

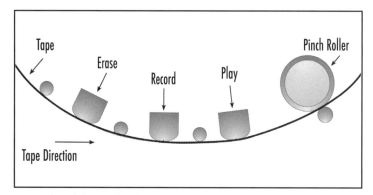

Tape slap delay utilized the distance between the record and playback heads. The recorder was set to record incoming signals but the play head was selected for playback. Tape speed and the distance between the heads determined the delay length.

fidelity, so each successive delay was duller. This created a very warm delay that was not intrusive on other mix ingredients. Modern plug-in delays are capable of maintaining identical audio quality indefinitely, but those full-quality repeats are distracting in many cases. Therefore, most delays provide an EQ that can tone down the high-frequency content of multiple delays so that they blend with the rest of the mix.

6. Doubling and tripling: Two more popular uses for a delay are the double and triple. Doubling uses a single delay between about 11 and 31 ms along with the source, frequently panned apart in the stereo spectrum. This technique is meant to simulate two performances of the same track, so there should be no regeneration. The exact delay time depends on the source sound, the desired amount of width in the mix, and the sound of the doubled track in mono. Any time short delays are combined—though they might sound great in stereo when panned apart—might also sound terrible in mono because of phase degradation; often the mono version sounds weak, thin, and quiet. This used to be a major concern when AM radio and television were mono mediums. However, today's biggest concern is usually how the recording will sound when played through a mono live sound system. Delays using prime numbers tend to yield the most consistent results between mono and stereo. When setting the delay time, either monitor the mix in mono or pan the two channels to the center, adjusting the delay time for the most natural and solid sound. Once the track is switched to stereo, it will still sound great, and you'll be able to trust that your doubled guitar sound won't disappear when you play the recording at your next gig. Tripling simply uses a stereo delay with two different delays within the same 11–31 ms range. It's most common to pan the two delays left and right while keeping the source track in the center position. As with doubling, set the exact times and positions while monitoring in mono.

7. Chorus, flanger, and phase shifter: All three of these effects combine a short delay of about 0.5–35 ms with the source track. The added ingredient that makes these effects different from simple doubling and slapback delays is the voltage controlled oscillator (VCO), which continuously sweeps the delay time below and above the specified delay. It should be noted that the VCO is actually speeding up and slowing down the source, so pitch variations are occurring. The depth control determines how extreme these pitch changes are, and longer delay times produce a much wider pitch range than short delay times. When combined with the source track, the sweeping delay causes rich and interesting changes in the overtones and harmonics that replicate the effect's name. A chorus uses the longest delay time around 35 ms, simulating the changes in time and pitch that happen naturally in a vocal choir. A flanger uses the same process as the chorus but within the 10–20 ms range. And the phase shifter also uses the same approach but within the 0.5–2 ms range.

TIP: Try equalizing or processing the delayed signal. Use a low-pass filter to remove the crisp highs on the delayed signal to help the delay blend better in the mix. Distortion, chorusing, flanging, and phase-shifting the delay creates a very interesting and compelling sound when used in the proper context.

OVERVIEW: Even though the commitment to exact delay effects and reverberation is typically left until mixdown, they are still very important during tracking because they help set the mood for the musicians. When musicians feel better about the way they sound, then they perform better. So, it's well worth the time and effort to set up monitor-only reverberation and delays to help inspire singers, guitarists, and so on. It's usually best to wait until mixdown to choose the best effects in context with the entire production. However, if you find a sound that works particularly well and truly inspires the musician's performance, either save a preset for that effect or record the effect alone without the source instrument to a separate stereo track.

CHALLENGE: During tracking, reverberation can inspire a great performance. However, when used in excess, it can also create a false sense of security for the musician. When the track is drowning in reverb, the end result is often a lazy performance because everything sounds so great to the musician. The goal in setting up the reverberation sound should be to provide just enough to inspire a great performance, but not so much that the result is less precise than it needs to be.

SOLUTION: Reverberation is a vast term that indicates a very wide range of sounds that mostly simulate naturally occurring acoustical spaces. However, with the ultimate control over almost any conceivable parameter provided by modern plug-ins, there are many options for outside-the-lines creativity when setting up sounds. To get the most out of reverberation devices, it's important to understand the following concepts:

1. What is reverberation? **Reverberation** is the combination of all of the discrete reflections of a sound source off all surfaces that are capable of reflecting the sound energy back to the listener. As you can imagine, a loud sound source in a concert hall could generate enough volume that countless discrete reflections from all conceivable angles—directly from the source and reflected around the room—could make their way back to the listener's ears. In fact, depending on the size of the room and the amount of energy created by the sound source, it could take several seconds for the reflections to die away.

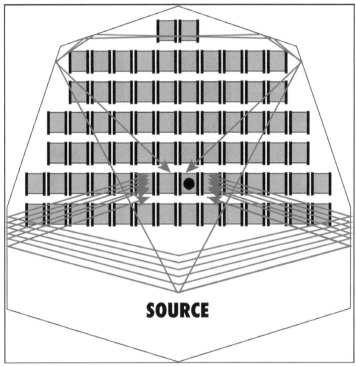

This illustration shows just a few of the millions of reflections that make up a natural reverberation sound.

2. Reverberation Time (**RT**): In an acoustical environment, the room size and acoustical treatment determine the reverberant decay time. The textbook definition of reverberation decay time is the amount of time it takes for the reverberation to decrease by 60 dB, often referred to as **T60**. Given similar acoustical treatment, large rooms generate longer reverberation times and small rooms generate shorter RTs. A typical T60 for a larger room is between 2 and 3 seconds.

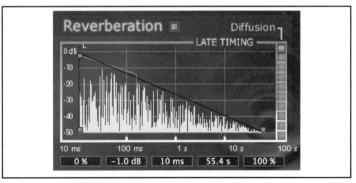

This great reverb plug-in is DreamVerb from UA. Its T60 is 55.4 seconds for illustration, but most T60s are between two and three seconds.

3. Predelay: This is one of the most powerful reverberation parameters. **Predelay** is an actual delay between the onset of the 100-percent dry source sound and the onset of the 100-percent wet reverberation. This important parameter allows for placement of the source sound in a room, either close to the listener or far away in the hall. Imagine that you are on the stage of a large concert hall while someone plays a violin at the far end of the hall. You'll hear the sound of the violin arriving along with all of the reverberant reflections from the entire room at a level similar or stronger than the violin—it will sound very far away from you as it arrives intertwined with the sound of the hall. Now, imagine yourself in the exact same hall in the same location on the stage, but the violinist plays while standing right in front of you. You hear the direct sound of the violin close to you, but behind that a little later, you hear the sound of the concert hall. The violin sounds intimate to you but also with the sound of the hall surrounding you. That's what the predelay does. It helps position the source close to the listener while still benefiting from the sound of the hall.

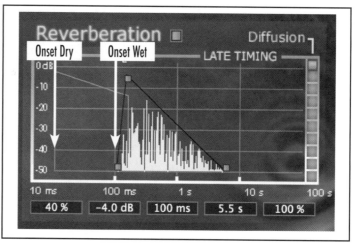

This Universal Audio DreamVerb screen shows that the reverberation starts 100 ms after the onset of the source.

4. Hall Reverb: Each of the reverberation types emulates the name describing the reverb. Hall reverb simulates the sound of a concert hall, which often has an RT of 2.5–3.5 seconds. This typically warm-sounding reverb has a characteristic roll-off in the high frequencies that helps the hall reverb blend well with a mix without excessive sibilance on vocals or distracting high-frequency shimmer.

5. Plate Reverb: Plate reverb usually contains the most high-frequency content of the reverb types. Keep in mind that modern reverberation plug-ins provide control of all available parameters, regardless of the basic category, so it is a simple matter to create a warm plate or a bright hall sound. A plate reverb emulates the sound created by an actual metal plate suspended in a metal frame by springs and placed in a wooden box, the most influential of which was the EMT 140 plate. A transducer at the center of the plate induces the source sound onto the plate, and then the sound of the plate vibration is picked up by two contact mics attached to the plate. Reverb time is controlled by physical dampeners that calm the plate's vibration.

6. Chamber Reverb: In a studio, reverberation chambers—usually called **echo chambers**—are actual acoustical spaces with a speaker at one end and a pair of high-quality condenser mics at the other. Bill Putnam, owner of Universal Audio, used the first chamber reverb on a Harmonicats recording of "Peg O' My Heart." The chamber was the studio bathroom. He went on to build actual chambers at his Chicago and Los Angeles studios. Chambers are typically a brick, stone, or concrete space coated with a highly reflective plaster.

7. Room Reverb: This type of reverberation simulates the sound of medium and small rooms. Room emulation is useful when building a unique-sounding reverb from multiple sounds. For example, using a small room sound on a snare drum helps provide life and interest to the basic sound that might not have originally existed. Then along with that, a hall reverb with a predelay a little longer than the RT of the room can help finish the sound.

8. Spring Reverb: Many vintage guitar amplifiers, such as the Fender Twin Reverb, include spring reverberation. The guitar sound stimulates an actual spring encased in metal, and sound from the vibration of the spring blends into the guitar sound. There are also studio versions of the spring reverb in which there are two separate canisters about 8 inches in diameter and 4 or 5 feet long that each contain a spring. The sound source is induced onto the spring, and the sound of both springs vibrating is routed back to the console for warm stereo sound.

TIP: Any large space can be used as a unique reverb chamber. In a commercial studio, it's common to send the source into the large studio room while capturing the room sound through two high-quality condenser mics. A church can provide a very unique and rich chamber sound as can a parking garage, empty grain silo, bathroom, or the cooling tower of an abandoned nuclear site.

GLOSSARY

A-weighted: a type of curve used to illustrate data in the measurement of sound pressure levels; A-weighting focuses on the frequency band that is associated with perceived volume and filters out the low band

Absorber: soft surfaces, such as foam, curtains, blankets, couches, and people generally absorb high frequencies; manufacturers such as Primacoustic, Auralex, and Acoustic Sciences design absorbers to address specific frequency bands, from broadband to low bands to mid and high bands

Active: a circuit that requires power to operate

Amperage: a term that refers to the strength of the electric current; units of amperage are called *amps*

Amplitude: a term that refers to the amount of energy in a waveform as reflected by the amount of positive and negative deviation from still air; amplitude only equates to perceived volume in a specific frequency range between about 1 and 4 kHz

Amp Simulator: syn. *amplifier simulator*; an electronic device or software application that recreates the inherent sound of modern and classic amplifiers, speakers, and sometimes the microphone used to capture the sound at the speaker

Auto-Pan: an effect that uses an oscillator to continuously pan the source signal back and forth across the stereo field

Baffle: a physical barrier used to isolate sound sources from other instruments in the same acoustic space; they often have a soft side to absorb sound and a hard side to reflect sound

Bidirectional Microphone: a microphone that captures sound equally from the front and back while leaving null points at 90 and 270 degrees off-axis in relation to the sound source

Blumlein Configuration: a coincident stereo miking technique that uses two bidirectional microphones aimed 90 degrees apart

C-weighted: a type of curve used to illustrate data in the measurement of sound pressure levels; C-weighted measurements indicate the overall amplitude of sound in an acoustical environment, registering a broad frequency range that is nearly flat across much of the audible band

Cardioid Microphone: a microphone with a heart-shaped polar pattern that captures sound primarily from the front of the mic while rejecting sounds produced from 180 degrees off-axis

Cent: a hundredth of a half-step interval

Chorus (effect): an effect that simulates the sounds of a choir, using a low frequency oscillator (LFO) to continuously modulate (vary) a 25–35 millisecond delay of a sound source played along with the original dry source; the depth and speed of the oscillation is used to control the strength and intensity of the effect

Coincident Technique: a stereo miking technique that uses two microphones on the same vertical and horizontal plane positioned as closely together as possible without touching, to minimize phase inconsistencies when the microphones are combined to a mono track, channel, or mix

Compression: a device that senses and decreases the difference between quiet and loud sounds

Condenser Microphone: a microphone in which a thinly coated plastic membrane vibrates in response to sound waves; the vibrations vary an area of electrically charged air particles, which is the origin of the audio signal provided by the microphone to the mixer; unlike the magnetic operating principles of dynamic and ribbon mic, condenser mics use an electrical operating principle and are considered the most accurate of the mic types

Delay: an effect that copies the sound at its input and repeats it, often in time intervals that match the song tempo in some way

Diaphragm: the component of any microphone that sympathetically vibrates in response to audio waves

Diffuser: a surface in an acoustical environment that redirects audio sound waves, typically with the designed purpose of minimizing standing waves that negatively color ambient sound

Digital Audio Workstation (DAW): a software-based audio recorder that is used to edit, record, produce, enhance, and manage files for audio productions

Digitally Controlled Attenuator (DCA): remotely controls a selected group of channels on a mixer. A DCA does not pass audio like a subgroup. It simply controls groups of faders that each pass audio.

Direct Box: also called a *direct injection* or just *DI*; a device that matches a high-impedance output, such as that from an electric guitar, to a low-impedance input, such as a mixer channel

Distortion: occurs when an audio input is overdriven

Dry: without an effect or processing

Dynamic Microphone: also called a *moving-coil* microphone; the dynamic capsule uses a plastic diaphragm attached to a cylinder of copper wire that is suspended around a magnet; the audio wave vibrates the diaphragm, moving the copper-wire cylinder around the magnet and varying the flow of north and south magnetism, which is the source of the microphone's output signal

Echo Chamber: reverberant acoustical space with a high-fidelity speaker on one end and pair of high-quality condenser microphones at the other; audio signals are sent to the speaker and the ambient sound from the mics is routed back into the mix on return channels

Equalization (EQ): the process of changing the balance of frequencies in an audio signal

Expander: a signal processor that increases dynamic range by decreasing the quiet parts of an audio signal, leaving the loudest audio unaffected

Flanger: an effect that produces a rich sweeping sound using a low frequency oscillator (LFO) to continuously modulate (vary) a 3–15 millisecond delay of a sound source played along with the original dry source; the depth and speed of the oscillation is used to control the strength and intensity of the effect

Gobo: see **baffle**

High-Pass Filter (HPF): an audio circuit that only lets the band above a specified frequency pass through unaffected, removing the low band below the specified frequency

Hypercardioid Microphone: a microphone that, like the cardioid microphone, captures sound primarily from the front but has decreased sensitivity at the sides and an area of decreased sensitivity about 110 degrees off-axis

Hysteresis: a phenomenon that occurs when the value of a physical proparty delays in relation to the effect causing the initial change.

Limiting: extreme compression using a ratio of 10:1 or above (often 100:1 or ∞:1) and a fast attack time

Low Frequency Oscillator (LFO): a circuit that continuously varies (oscillates) an audio parameter above and below its normal state; the LFO is frequently used to oscillate timing, tone, or timbre

Mid-Side (MS) Configuration: a stereo miking technique that combines a cardioid microphone and a bidirectional microphone with its side aimed at the source; in the MS circuit the bidirectional side mic is panned hard to one side and the same signal is split and sent to another channel, reversed in polarity, and panned hard to the other side for a wide stereo sound that collapses perfectly to mono

Noise Gate: an effect that turns the signal off when it is below a user-adjusted threshold

Omnidirectional Microphone: a microphone that does not reject sound from any direction in a 360-degree sphere around the mic capsule

ORTF Configuration: a stereo miking technique developed by the *Office de Radiodiffusion Télévision Francaise* that positions two cardioid microphones with their capsules 17 cm apart and aimed between 90 and 110 degrees apart

Passive: a circuit that does not require power to operate

Phantom Power: 48-volt DC power supplied by a battery or, more commonly, from the mixer's XLR input to the active microphone or direct box

Phase Coherence: a constant phase relationship between two or more devices; phase-coherent audio signals share the same phase and sum to mono in way that sounds full and clear

Phase Shifter: an effect that produces a rich sweeping sound using a low frequency oscillator (LFO) to continuously modulate (vary) a delay of about 0.5–2 milliseconds of the sound source played along with the original dry source; the depth and speed of the oscillation is used to control the strength and intensity of the effect

Polar Pattern: a visual representation of microphone directionality

Polarity: a waveform's voltage position above or below an established midpoint

Pop Filter: see **windscreen**

Predelay: the time delay between the dry audio source and the onset of the 100-percent wet reverberation

Proximity Effect: the phenomenon whereby low frequencies become relatively stronger compared to high frequencies as the microphone is moved closer to the sound source

Reamping: recording the sound of a recorded track being played back through an amplifier

Regeneration: routing the delay output back into the delay input, adjusting the number of repeats of the delay by varying the strength of the delayed signal; used to increase the number of delays from one to infinity (∞)

Reverberation (effect): an effect that uses mathematical algorithms to generate many discrete delays that simulate the reflections in a natural or contrived acoustical environment

Reverberation (acoustic): the combination of all of the discrete reflections of a sound source off all surfaces that are capable of reflecting sound energy back to listener

Reverberation Time (RT): the amount of time it takes for the reverberation to decrease by 60 dB (termed as **T60**)

Ribbon Microphone: a microphone in which an audio wave vibrates a thin metal ribbon suspended in a magnetic field, causing a variation in the north-south magnetism that is the source of the mic signal; ribbon mics are known for their warm, smooth sound quality

Screen: see **baffle**

Sibilance: in speech or singing, consonant sounds, such as "s," "sh," "t," or "ch" that produce a focused hissing sound

Slapback: a delay effect in which a single delayed playback of the original source sound is generated; the regeneration control is often used to create multiple repeats of the slapback delay

Sound Pressure Level (SPL): the measured energy contained in an audio waveform

Spaced Omni Pair Configuration: a stereo miking technique that uses two omnidirectional microphones in front of a sound source, spaced between 3 and 10 feet apart

Summing: the process by which multiple audio channels are electronically routed together, such as when creating mixdown stems, when a stereo image is collapsed to a mono, or when bouncing a surround, stereo, or mono mixdown

Supercardioid Microphone: a microphone that, like the cardioid microphone, captures sound primarily from the front but has decreased sensitivity at the sides and an area of decreased sensitivity about 170 degrees off-axis

3:1 Rule: a miking principle stating that the distance between any two microphones used in the same acoustical environment must be separated by at least three times the distance from each mic to its intended source

Transient: a fast initial attack, exceeding the average level by up to 9 dB or more, produced when an instrument is struck with a hard surface; drums and cymbals played with sticks, percussion instruments, pianos, and acoustic guitars played with a pick all produce a transient

Volt: the force that pushes the current—a unit of electrical potential; a volt represents the strength of the force behind the current, whereas amps represent the speed of the current.

Voltage Controlled Amplifier (VCA): an amplifying circuit that raises and lowers the signal level in response to increases and decreases in voltage

Voltage Controlled Oscillator (VCO): a device that raises and lowers frequency in response to increases and decreases in voltage

Wattage: the power generated by the product of voltage (electric potential) and amperage (electric current); units of wattage are called *watts*

Windscreen: a device positioned between the vocalist and the microphone that uses acoustically transparent foam or nylon mesh to minimize excessive air movement caused by plosive sounds onto the microphone diaphragm; also called a *pop filter*

X-Y Configuration: a coincident technique that uses two cardioid microphones with their capsules as close together as possible, aimed across the same physical plane, and positioned at a 90-degree angle to each other

ABOUT THE AUTHOR

Bill Gibson (SEATTLE), president of Northwest Music and Recording, Inc., instructor at Berklee College of Music Online, and respected author has spent his lauded career writing, recording, producing, and teaching music. As a veteran audio professional, active sound engineer, and video producer, Bill has developed unique insights into the techniques and procedures that produce extremely high-quality audio, both in the recording studio and in live performances. He has written and produced over 40 books and countless instructional videos, all acclaimed for their straightforward and understandable explanations of audio concepts and applications.

Gibson has written and developed a wide range of instructional content alongside some of the music industry's most iconic professionals, including Quincy Jones (*The Quincy Jones Legacy Series: Q on Producing*), Bruce Swedien (*The Bruce Swedien Recording Method*), Dave Pensado (*The Pensado Papers*), Sylvia Massy (*Recording Unhinged: Creative and Unconventional Recording Techniques*), and Al Schmitt (*Al Schmitt on Vocal and Instrumental Recording Techniques* and *Al Schmitt On the Record: The Magic Behind the Music*). He has also authored publications under his own name, which include the six-volume *Hal Leonard Recording Method*, *The Ultimate Live Sound Operator's Handbook*, *The Ultimate Church Sound Operator's Handbook*, and many more!

As a two-term National Trustee, a member of the National Advisory Committee for the Producers & Engineers Wing and the Planning & Governance Committee, and as a Governor for the Pacific Northwest Chapter of The Recording Academy, Gibson advocates for the benefit of music producers, technicians, and performers locally, regionally, nationally, and internationally. He also authored "Recommendations for High-Resolution Music Production" for the Recording Academy's Producers & Engineers Wing along with committee members Leslie Ann Jones, Chuck Ainlay, Bob Ludwig, Rick Plushner, and Phil Wagner.